SPLIT-CANE AND SABLE

Also by Robin Armstrong
THE PAINTED STREAM

SPLIT-CANE AND SABLE

A book of Fish, Men and Nature

Robin Armstrong

J.M. DENT & SONS LTD
London & Melbourne

First published 1988
© Robin Armstrong 1988

Printed in Great Britain by
Butler & Tanner Ltd, Frome and London
for J M Dent & Sons Ltd
91, Clapham High Street, London SW4 7TA

This book is set in 11/13½ Linotron Palatino by
Gee Graphics Ltd, Crayford, Kent

British Library Cataloguing in Publication Data

Armstrong, Robin
    Split cane and sable : a book of men and nature.
    1. Fishing — England — Devon
    I. Title
    799. 1'1'0924   SH606

    ISBN 0-460-04745-0

Contents

Acknowledgements

I should like to thank the following people for help in the preparation of this book:

Oliver Swann for his help and advice in selecting picture subjects.
David and Tania Channing-Williams for trusting me not to take their name in vain.
Nick Marchant-Lane for his advice, friendship and support.

Derek Maw, Brian Harris, Keith Linsell and Tony Johnson for the hours of fun remembered.

And lastly and above all Bob Speddy.

ROBIN ARMSTRONG
Woodtown Cottage — October 1987

Introduction

Over thirty years ago, I bought a brightly painted, balsa-wood float from a market stall in the East End of London. I had no idea what it was, nor how I should ever use it, but its shape, colour and feel entranced me. I knew, with boyish certainty, that it would prove to be the luckiest and most powerful of talismans. And I was right. That float was to lead me to all the delights of rural life in some of the loveliest parts of Britain.

This book is about part of that life. It celebrates fishing and painting, and people who fish and some of the places where they fish. It sketches the erratic progress of a passionate angler from his first grubby perch in North London to the sweet brown trout of his middle-life on the edge of Dartmoor. On the way, it calls on Kentish carp and Dungeness cod; on Sussex bass and Scottish herring; on some of nature's fishermen, and on the pleasures of collecting classic tackle.

If this gentle discourse on some aspects of an angler's life and art awakens interest in the uncommitted, encourages the novice and stirs pleasurable memories in the veteran, it will have achieved its purpose.

1

Jellied Eels and Wary Perch

North London is hardly the place to learn to fish. There are no salmon rivers running merrily alongside the Balls Pond Road, and trout streams, to the best of my remembrance, are very rare. In Dalston Junction, where I spent part of my childhood, the fishing season passes almost unnoticed, and the few birds which sing are rapidly gobbled up by mangy cats. There is a marked lack of interest in the habits of coot and tern, and some local citizens believe that England would be a better place if it were paved over from Tweed to Fal. A river, in their view, is a place for dumping old bicycles.

I didn't actually live in North London. My home was a council house in St Paul's Cray, in Kent, to which dismal exile we had been moved after a bombed-out spell in a rest home near Bromley-by-Bow. The family spent time north of the Thames only because my favourite aunt, Aunt Lil, was landlady of a splendid pub, the Talbot, and my parents often acted as her weekend assistants.

The Talbot was a genuine, no-nonsense, Victorian brass and mahogany drinking house where people went, unashamedly, to have a good time. It had tables with proper marble tops and wrought-iron legs too heavy to push over except in anger. The top halves of the doors were of opaque glass engraved with words like 'smoking room' and 'private bar', and three dart boards, side by side, catered for the in-house entertainment. All the customers seemed extremely robust: the men swigged pints from straight glasses, and the women disposed of large gins with great ease and no apparent thought of an overweight tomorrow.

The Talbot smelled of jellied eels, pickled walnuts and stale beer. Pints were drawn from hand-pumps linked to the cellar, and on an average Saturday it was almost impossible to see from one end of the bar to the other through the cigarette smoke. It was rumoured that a wheelbarrow stood in the backyard ready to push home those patrons who were unable to walk.

To a child of ten or eleven, the Talbot seemed enormous, and overwhelming. The function room upstairs on the first floor always seemed to be full of people arguing, singing, dancing and, above all, drinking. My aunt told me that sometimes they laid out the main guest in a coffin and drank until they were ready to bury him, but I never believed her. On reflection, however, she may have been telling the truth: wakes, in those days, were not uncommon.

I remember summer days filled with the sharp tang of petrol and hot tar. My senses were attuned to traffic noise and the smell of musty tap rooms, not to bird-song and meadowsweet: no wistaria trailed in from the wide window of my cramped bedroom, and there was no terrace from which my father called me down to ride. I don't remember many autumn leaves, or daffodils dancing in the spring breezes. Flowers were dull tulips in regimented rows in Finsbury Park, or things you bought from barrows. It hardly occurred to me that people grew their own, in gardens. The only things my aunt ever grew were hyacinth bulbs in a cupboard under the stairs, and a small moustache, as she got older, on her upper lip.

But I do not complain of deprivation. My childhood was lively and filled with freedom. Dalston Junction was really a village: a big, noisy, dirty, bustling village, a safe place for children, friendly and generous. It was like living in a very extended family, since the old society had not then dissolved nor proceeded upward on its mobile way to the suburbs. The good, the bad, the lawful and the unlawful lived side by side, if not in amity at least in armed truce. And in the middle of it all, I was being brought up by a loving family. Despite some squalors and overcrowding, the environment was rich in character and large in spirit. I could think of many worse places in which to grow.

When I look back, I realise that I must have spent more time in St Paul's Cray than in Dalston, for St Paul's Cray was where I lived and went to school. But it was Dalston, and the times spent exploring its excitements with my cousin Chris, that I remember best.

Chris was more daring than I. He was the local boy and I was the country cousin to whom he uncovered all the wonders of the bustling Saturday streets, and the stalls at the Waste, half a mile away. Hip-high to most adults, we wandered amid a forest of legs, eagerly examining what was on offer within the range of our limited pocket-money.

In Waste Market stalls supplied almost every human and domestic need. You could buy everything from cheap knickers to artificial fur coats by way of tawdry household utensils and toys which broke almost before you got them home. One large lady sold sarsaparilla by the glass and usually gave us one free, while another lady, equally ample and amiable, made apple fritters, cored and cut into rings, like doughnuts, and cooked in a great pan of boiling oil. But above all other stalls was the one which sold bits and pieces of fishing tackle.

I wasn't sure at first what the stuff was, but the shapes and colours and complications of it all intrigued me: I was drawn to the stall like a fly to sticky paper. Here I bought my first float, made from balsa wood, beautifully shaped and painted in yellow and black with a red tip.

Both my parents and Chris thought me mad to waste precious pocket-money on buying it. But it sustained and comforted me. I didn't know what it was really for, but it was my lucky charm, prized above all others, and I carried it with me everywhere, obsessively, as children do. I still have it, carefully tucked away, and fellow-fishermen will surely understand why.

That float, hand-made from balsa wood

Apart from the tackle stall, we were also drawn to the place which sold jellied eels. We would watch the owner take the wriggling creatures out of a glass water-tank and decapitate them, in deft chops, on a battered old bread-board. There was also a pie-and-mash shop in the market, Manze's I think it was called, which stirred in me that form of desperate hunger which only afflicts children. It was a marvellous place, lined with old-fashioned tiles and full of people feasting on meat pies topped with dollops of creamy potato covered in parsley sauce and liberally drenched in malt vinegar. I determined that when I became rich, I would dine off nothing else, every day.

But I have more than gastronomic memories of Manze's since it was there that I met the man who unwittingly shaped the whole of my future.

'Where do you fish, sonny?' he asked me, as he saw me playing with the float. 'Clissold or Finsbury Park?'

'Fish?' I couldn't properly understand the question, not knowing its connection with my float.

My questioner was patient. Adults and children seemed to talk together, at least in the East End, rather more then than they do

The float that started me off

Robin Armstrong '87.

Wary perch

now. He soon realised my ignorance. 'Look,' he said, 'I run the tackle stall. You probably bought that float from me. But you'll get more fun out of fishing than just messing about with it. Come back to the stall and I'll fix you up with some gear.'

I had no money. No matter, he said, I could have the stuff as a present. He then gave me a wireless aerial from an old tank, made up as a rod; half a line; an old reel, and a few hooks.

'Right!' he said. 'Get yourself round to Finsbury Park ponds; watch what the others do and you'll soon be a fisherman.'

Minnow — every boy's start in angling

Like all the best Dads, my father could always make time for his importunate son. The following week, he took me to Finsbury Park, an archetypal municipal playground, complete with spiked iron railings, notices banning almost every worthwhile human activity, and a cadre of old park-keepers in peaked caps who could never hope to outrun the young malefactors who continually defied their shaking sticks. Only the halt, the lame and the very weedy failed to escape them, although none of us dared to approach them too closely. Their presence at least maintained some sort of order.

The pond to which my father took me, he as ignorant as I about what we should do when we got there, was murky and unattractive. There was a small island in the middle of it which served as a refuge for a dismal band of overweight swans and ducks: every so often, one or two would risk a sortie onto the water to pick up food thrown by harassed mothers desperately trying to divert their screaming children. Compared with their cousins in the wild, these birds were well nourished, but that hardly made them more attractive. They were so full of bread rolls and old buns that they could hardly stagger. It took a lot of waddle for them to get airborne, and when they finally achieved lift-off, their flights were short and graceless. Most of them took to leaving the island, I suspect, only after the Park had closed at night and the children who threw stones or cast lines at them had tired of their sport.

At Mount House Preparatory School, Tavistock, near where I now live, gilded lads of eleven or twelve learn to cast, under the sharp eye of an expert salmon fisherman, on the school lake. The old school buildings sparkle in the sunlight and the grounds reach out to the eye in a wealth of greenery. You can hear the traditional sound of leather against willow and the tinkle of cups as Matron sets out the cricket tea. It is a long way from North London and the Finsbury Park Academy of Piscatorial Science. I learned the beginnings of fishing from watching the boys who stood near by me, and imitating them. It was weeks before I could control the line at the end of my tank aerial, and stop it from becoming entangled in the iron railings or the bushes behind me, and weeks before I became an accepted member of the group which crowded the limited catchment area of that public pond. But I finally established myself as a serious, if not very skilled angler, and eventually I experienced the thrill of my first bite.

The float went down into the dark waters in a manner I had learned from observing the others. But the perch below was smarter than I was. He and his fellows were so pestered that they had become too wise to be hooked. He escaped. I suspect that the only ones who allowed themselves to be caught there were those overtaken by a death wish, who had decided that life in such soot-filled surroundings was not worth living any longer.

But fishing is fishing, and enjoyment is never absent from its pursuit: even if the Finsbury Park perch bore little resemblance to his succulent cousin in some monastery garden, he was a worthwhile quarry. When I finally caught one, I was delighted. In one movement, I hooked him and propelled him straight over my shoulder onto the grass behind me. I had finally caught something.

The perch, looking rather smaller than I had fancied it, lay twitching. I was by no means sure what to do with it. Stretching my hand out with the intention of killing it, I scratched my palm on the sharp spines of its fins. It was painful, and I cried out. Just then, a man strolled over from where he had been sitting, silent and still, with two rods on twin rod rests, further down the side of the pond. 'You don't want that, son,' he said. 'You'll get far more fun from putting it back and catching it again than from taking it home.' I recognised later, but not at the time, that he was probably a specimen hunter, one of a very rare and special breed, out for a carp perhaps; just then, he seemed to me to be mad. What was the point of catching a fish only to throw it back?

But I did as he suggested. In those days, small boys tended to do what they were told, especially when they were told by large, dour men of some authority. But I was resentful, and it took me a long time to realise that one could catch fish and lose nothing of one's pleasure by throwing them back.

At home in St Paul's Cray, the nearest public place to fish was Chislehurst, rather a long walk away for a twelve-year-old on his own, so I usually only went there with Derek Maw, a friend who had begun to fish as avidly as I had. Stopping there once on our way back from Eltham Baths, we found a dried-up pool, lined and cracked like a rain-starved African water hole. All it lacked was the presence of a thirsty lion. There was one place only, right in the middle, which was still wet. I plunged my hand in and, groping about, felt something scaly. I pulled it out and it proved to be a crucian carp, about ½lb in weight. It was big, compared with the puny perch I knew from Finsbury Pond, and we were both excited when we located five more.

We took them home, wrapped, to the horror of my mother, in my new artificial leather jacket. She was even more upset when I displayed them on her newly polished back step. Eventually my father filled an old tin bath with water and we put them in that. To our surprise, they wriggled back to life, and Derek and I, not noted as keen students at school, became embryo zoologists overnight. Alas, our pretensions to expertise on the behaviour of the carp came to nought. Thinking to improve their environment, we stole some gravel from a building site and sprinkled it liberally into the bath-tub. Next morning, the fish were dead, victims no doubt of chemically treated stones.

Chislehurst ponds yielded mainly sticklebacks and an occasional perch. I found them devoid of charm, and I only sparked again into proper fishing life when I became old enough to get to the River Darent in Kent. This is one of the only three chalk streams I have ever fished, although then I was not fishing it as a chalk stream: I was simply one of a gang of urchins, looking for gudgeon and minnows, and still using my old tank aerial as a rod.

The park at Eynsford, north of Maidstone, through which the Darent made its relatively rustic way, was green and leafy. A poet in search of inspiration would undoubtedly find it more rewarding than Finsbury. The strollers were better dressed and more relaxed than their London equivalents. There were chestnut and willow trees trailing down to the water's edge and, although I was too concerned with fishing to notice them, I have no doubt that doves were cooing somewhere in the immemorial elms. It was a placid place, very English, and I found little wrong with it except that the fishing on either side of the park was private and out of reach.

Derek and I — he lordly, with his brand-new Milbro rod — would make our way there from St Paul's Cray by train or bicycle whenever we could, drawn by the knowledge that trout were always escaping from the private water on each side of the public fishing spot. Sooner or later, we felt, one would fall to us. By now, we were both becoming quite skilled: when our opportunity arrived, we would be ready for it.

The day my float rushed upstream at the speed of light, I had enough experience to know that it wasn't being towed by a gudgeon. That stolid denizen of the Eynsford deeps would have kept on munching. I knew that I must have met my first trout,

Pollard willow — memories of Eynsford

and my emotions were all I had ever expected they would be. When I finally landed a beautiful brownie, I felt like a hero, and most of my fellows, accustomed to minnows, treated me like one.

When I took it home, filled with new pride, my father was keen to have it mounted. The cost proved too much, and my first real catch was eaten. From that moment on, fishing became an obsession. I went back to Eynsford as often as I could, and began to take in Shoreham and Otford, which were previously out of bounds. I began to catch dace, and roach and chub which had escaped from various ponds, and slowly my tally began to build up. I was becoming a competent fisherman, but my old tank aerial, bent and bruised by various battles with determined trout, grew ever more of an embarrassment. I 'lost' it, and told my father it had been stolen, The guilt lies with me still.

I am certain my father knew what I had done. But he said nothing. Next morning, he took me to the smart tackle shop in St Mary Cray and allowed me to choose a proper three-piece cane rod. I think I was about thirteen. At that moment, I knew that no boy in Britain had a better father. And that no boy in Britain was happier than I was.

Great crested grebe on nest

2
Pilgrim's Progress

Derek Maw and I graduated from our Eynsford elysium in 1958. We were now old enough to travel further afield, and we had set our new fishing ambitions on the streams and hammer-ponds surrounding Denton, the village near Newhaven in Sussex, where we stayed during the holidays with Derek's hospitable and tolerant grandparents. Later, from the same base, we were to extend our activities to include the estuary, pier, and neighbouring beaches.

Eynsford had been blissful enough, but we had grown out of it. We were now initiates, or so we thought; practised fishermen who could hold their own along with the best of the old hands. We firmly, if falsely, believed that our apprenticeships in the angling arts were almost over.

If the beginning of wisdom is the recognition of one's ignorance, then we began to acquire wisdom in the months that followed. We found that we had much to learn. Chislehurst and Eynsford turned out to have been mere nursery schools. Our real education began when we tried for the rudd and perch of the hammer-ponds*, and for the mullet and bass which cruised the tidal waters of the town pier. Newhaven, and the countryside around it, not then so busy as now, was to become our College of Further Fishing Education, and we studied there with zest.

Meanwhile, Sussex-by-the-Sea and its tidy villages lay open to us. I looked out of the train windows onto a very different world from that of St Paul's Cray. Everything was lusher and more at ease. Great trees sat comfortably in green fields: at home, ours vied apologetically with burgeoning concrete, as though they knew that the contractor's men would soon come to cut them down and root them out.

Red-backed male shrike — the 'butcher bird'

Nothing in St Paul's Cray was then allowed to stand in the way of new building. I remember watching, with sadness, as bulldozers shoved aside the last hedgerow: the previous day, quite by chance, I had seen there the nest of a red-backed shrike, the 'butcher bird', surrounded by its grisly larder of assorted prey, impaled on spikes of bramble and blackthorn. I had read

*When Sussex was a centre of iron-making, streams were impounded to create hammer-ponds to work the bellows for the forges.

somewhere that there were very few breeding pairs of shrike in the whole country, and I doubted if the children who came after me on this brave new estate would ever see any of them.

In Sussex, houses stood as naturally as the woodlands which surrounded them. They were warm and weathered and set in old gardens, bursting with blossom: they were places to live in, not mere shelters in which to take refuge after the storms of a tedious day. They were friendly and welcoming and very English: they had leaded windows, open to the sun, and paddocks where pink-faced girls in jodhpurs coaxed sleek ponies over artificial jumps. Had I been a more social and political animal, I might have envied those who lived in these flintstone Edens.

Even the birds seemed to sing more sweetly in Sussex than in North Kent, where sooty starlings, graceless and unkempt, were the main ornithological attraction. For an aspiring artist and naturalist, Sussex was a magical place. The variety of wildlife, from the chalkhill blues of the Downs to the sea-birds of the coast, was a constant inspiration. The habitat around Denton contained more than enough subjects to beguile and entrance a schoolboy: it provided everything I could hope for. The long summer days seemed to go on for ever, and when Derek and I finally sank into our happy beds, we were replete with happiness; and, very often, with a fish supper.

In the beginning, we concentrated on the hammer-ponds and streams. Most of them were free of people, for cars in those days were beyond the reach of most families. Visitors came mainly by train, and stayed on the beaches or the sea-front. Our excursions into the byways and secret places away from the town were unspoilt by company: nobody bothered us and, until we took to sea-fishing from the pier, we spent most of our time on our own.

They were good and innocent days. At first we mainly caught rudd and perch, learning our sporting trade as we went along. Occasionally, I would go after some solitary old perch whom I suspected of residing, alone and broodingly, in a reed bed. This entailed using a Wye* lead, fitted about a foot above a small,

*So called because it is commonly used in spinning for salmon on the River Wye.

green plug as the lure, then casting alongside the reed-bed so that the buoyant plug would float and bob attractively (I hoped) above the weight, and not get entangled in the vegetation below. I couldn't see my fish, but I imagined him blundering through the subterranean forest of reeds, unaware of what awaited him. At the right moment, and it was never easy to decide when this had come, I would bring him out with a fast retriever and a series of short snatches. Indeed, the best perch I ever caught anywhere was by this method. It was a 3½-pounder which I proudly delivered into the skilful culinary hands of Derek's grandmother: normally we put back most of what we caught, having learned not to carry off, unnecessarily, that which we did not intend to eat.

I've lost count of how many eels I've caught

The eels were even more intractable, for a small boy, than the perch. They were all female, stubborn and muscled like old-fashioned washerwomen, and we caught them by mounting small rudd with baiting needles onto large hooks. They used to grow to three or four pounds in weight; they were hard to catch, and even harder to land. Often, like miniature boa constrictors, they would wrap their strong tails round the nearest obstacle.

With our frail and makeshift tackle, they were not easy to move. Those we did land, we mostly threw back; though for a lad brought up in the cockney tradition of jellied eels, it was difficult not to take the odd one for the pot. Nowadays, I doubt if the same waters are quite so fecund.

Derek and I were more than satisfied with our hobby. He, too, was a bird-watcher and naturalist: he, too, found contentment in an environment which was then less threatened than now by the pressures of new housing and large numbers of visitors. Apart from using slightly different tackle, we probably fished much as boys might have done in the previous century, and caught just as much. Today, alas, the places where schoolboys can roam freely are limited, and the catches they can expect, except from artificially stocked lakes, are less encouraging than those which we knew. Even sea-fishing now yields many fewer rewards than it did: the bass is relatively rare, and for a boy to catch one from a south-coast pier would be a prize indeed.

We began our sea-fishing off Newhaven and the River Cuckmere, attracted by the mullet which then came up the estuaries. To us they were just another fish, albeit a sea-fish, but we had been told that many anglers found them almost impossible to catch. Intensive shoal-fish, they were said to filter through the algae, weed and organic matter on which they fed, at terrific speed. Local men told us that you had to be very quick to strike in order to take them.

This proved to be true. But our previous coarse-fishing experience with the fast-biting roach and rudd and, to a lesser extent, bream and perch, helped us greatly. So, oddly enough, did our lack of proper sea-tackle: the three-piece tip action rods we then used proved to be ideal for our new sport. We both became adept at reacting to a quickly dipping float by striking even faster.

Brian Harris, sometime editor of *Angling* and an expert on this fish, recommends an Avon rod with a middle action which, I think, is right for the fighting qualities of mullet. But at that time we had no choice. We simply used the rods we had with a four-pound line, an ordinary float and shot rig and a decent-sized hook. And with these, and our special bait, we caught as many as we could wish.

The special bait was banana, said by mullet men to be deadly. To have told Derek's grandmother that we wanted bananas to use as bait would have been sacrilege. So we simply asked if we could have banana sandwiches for our packed lunches, and it was these, rolled between our fingers into a paste, that we launched as groundbait. It was an unlikely attraction but, on the Cuckmere, it worked. We used it as hook bait, although in the gritty and salty water, it was difficult to keep on.

Sanderling at rest

In time, either the supply of banana sandwiches must have dried up or our hunger must have become more exigent, for we began to eat our sandwiches instead, and turned, successfully, to the rag worms commonly found in all Sussex harbours. They were expensive to buy, so we laboriously dug our own, toiling through piles of thick, clinging Cuckmere mud and ooze to reach them. It was very dirty work, but they made excellent bait.

When we fished in the open sea, we used lug worms from revealed sand, nicknaming them, because of their submarine shape, 'lugmarines'. It was hardly a brilliant invention, but the word was all of a piece with the secret world which schoolboys like to create for themselves. Who else knew what 'lugmarines' were? Even adult anglers would not immediately connect them with the creatures they used as bait. Our private term set us apart and made us different. In the great Brotherhood of the Angle, we had our own small and special lodge.

A mullet of three pounds looked huge to us but, provided you didn't spook the shoal, and could keep them on the feed, you could go on catching them for ever. This was joy indeed. As that first sea-fishing summer wore on, we became veritable Masters of the Mullet; experts in its quicksilver ways; mullet men supreme; genuine fishermen. For catching mullet demanded high skills. You had to strike deftly, bring your fish to the edge of its shoal and then follow it through its fast runs. It taught me not only good angling sense, but grounded me in techniques which apply, almost interchangeably, to all other branches of the angler's art.

Most of our mullet we returned. But occasionally we kept one which Derek's grandmother would soak in brine, to remove the estuary mud, and then cook. What she cooked it with, I do not know, but like most fish it always tasted good. I have heard that grey mullet can be served with bacon and eggs, as well as with grapes and white wine, but I cannot imagine that was the way we ate it. But when you are a schoolboy, and you have caught your own supper, you enjoy it however it is served.

Estuary mullet led us, inexorably, to pier-fishing. The ferries then were less frequent than now and Newhaven harbour was less washed by the continual passage of ships rushing over to Dieppe. The world was younger, and it was still possible to find succulent bass in some numbers. And once Derek's grandmother had performed her culinary wonders on our first specimen we judged it the most delicious fish we had ever eaten, and were determined to catch more.

Our equipment was now more appropriate to our advancing status. We had progressed from boys' gear to what, in our early-teen eyes, was properly adult: two-piece, solid glass spinning rods, nicely suited to the pier-fishing on which we now intended to concentrate. All we now needed was some rudimentary tuition in the art we had elected to follow.

We got this not from books, but by watching and pestering a local expert who, we thought, seemed to know everything that one man could possibly know about the ways and wiles of those bass which decided, unluckily, to come anywhere near Newhaven. He was a weatherbeaten, leather-faced man, with an old flat cap and a tweed jacket caked in fish scales and slime. We could smell him, if the wind was right, before we could see him. We never learned his name, nor where he had developed his unique skills, but we guessed he had spent most of his life in Newhaven, sitting on the same spot on the same pier ever since he was a boy, doing nothing but fish.

Our Professor, which is what, for the sake of his own peace, he had somewhat reluctantly become, favoured gear which was slightly old-fashioned even then. He had an ancient, ten-foot Hardy split-cane, salmon spinning rod, which he regularly plied, and very successfully, at the lowest seaward side of the inner pier. His sliding float was usually adjusted to leave his hook many feet below the water surface (though he varied the depth with the state of the tide) and his bait was always a live prawn, taken from the stock he carried with him in an old cough-sweet tin. To keep the prawns fresh, the tin had holes in the top and was left suspended in the sea by an old rope.

The prawn would be hooked round its body in the usual way and then, not casting, the Professor would lower it gently into the sea, close by the harbour wall. Had he cast, he would have lost this fragile bait and that, as he kept telling us testily, as we continually appealed to him when one of our own disappeared, was 'criminal'. Prawns were easy to lose, but hard to find: if we were going to be proper fishermen, we should learn not to waste them. He himself nurtured a stock of prawns in a tub of sea-water outside his terrace house in Station Road, but he didn't keep them 'to give away to careless boys'.

Meanwhile, he continued to instruct us. He would lower his bait at the lowest point of the tide, theorising that the bass would be roaming round the piling and the ships moored in the harbour, feeding on the bits of live food washed out by the tide when it came on the make. These movements gave life to his own bait, and allowed him, with no great effort, to take in four- or five-pound fish with great regularity.

The Professor also taught us that bass needed time to engulf and absorb the whole prawn. Strike early, and you would lose it. 'Watch the float go down and count thirty before you strike,' he said, but we found it hard to be so patient. It took us a while to heed his sensible admonition.

Bass, as I would imagine one lurking around Newhaven pier

Although I was not aware of the similarity at the time, I suppose it was a bit like fishing for pike, but whether the old man had graduated earlier from freshwater angling, we never discovered. We simply watched and listened and felt grateful for his introduction to such good fishing.

We never actually tired of the pier, but we did gradually begin to explore further afield. Wandering along the beach between Newhaven and Seaford, we had seen people casting into the surf and thought we ought to try doing the same. No matter that we lacked the right equipment; we had enthusiasm, and an infinite capacity for learning new tricks. Soon, we were experimenting from a stretch known as the Buckle, a piece of shingle which was particularly productive, and where we were lucky enough to meet yet another generous teacher, Jack Austin.

Jack showed us bass which today's beach-fishermen, or even today's housewives, sadly surveying the pathetic tables of their local fishmonger, rarely see. His advice was brief, and pointed. 'Try after the storm,' he would say, 'Just beyond the first breaker. That's where the bass will be, sniffing about for food stirred up by the rough seas.' And so they were, just as he said they would be.

But we did not get them without a fight. With our light tackle we were touching the limits of fishing possibility with spinning rods. But it was great fun, and being small boys was no great disadvantage because we found more fish near the limits of our reach than there were further out. On many occasions we took more than the professional-looking men with their huge rods who stood alongside us.

We used (not truly from choice, because our means were restricted to what we had) a three-ounce bullet weight and a normal ledger link between swivel and hook on a flowing trace. With this, we would cast into the breakers and bounce the bullet along the troughs. In the early days, we baited with lugworm, then with frozen squid, but the best bait of all was a huge sandwich of slipper limpets, piled on through their muscles so that they didn't slip off the hook. The upper part of the beach was littered with this convenient fish-food, washed over from the Continent, and we used it by the hundredweight.

'Big bait, big bass,' said the stolid yeomen of Sussex who fished with us, and we were loath to disagree with them. Sometimes we used nine to ten limpets to a hook, and it was always easy to tell where we had been all day by the piles of empty shells lying beside our dugout in the shingle, which we built to protect us from the worst of the gales.

Whatever else changes, English summers do not. Blue skies turned to cloud just as capriciously as they do now, and harsh winds brought out the red No Bathing flags with the same regularity. Our days were not all spent in sunshine. But the

Newhaven Rudd
Robin Armstrong '87

Broadland pike

Male common blue x 2

weather hardly bothered us. Nor did any lack of fishing success. It was enough to be on the beach, tasting the salt spray, watching the gulls wheeling and screaming over the cliffs, and checking the ever-moving and changing sea.

As the days wore on we widened our ambitions towards other fish, notably mackerel. We would watch the gulls for signs of feeding shoals, then attack them in the traditional float-fishing manner, with a sliding float pre-set to a depth of three or four feet, depending on what we saw, and take whatever came. As bait we used brit*, if we could get it, and thin slices of flesh cut from the side of a mackerel if we could not. Sometimes we would just spin amid the shoal with a German sprat lure shaped like a spoon handle, all brilliant and shiny.

All these pelagic fish — mackerel, garfish and bass — are great fighters, because they feed on the move and move very fast. Often, rather than use the German sprat, I preferred a float, watching it disappear amid the mêlée of fish and diving birds, not knowing what I was about to take. But shoals of this kind are

*The local name for the young of herring or sprat.

21

rarely seen nowadays: perhaps, even, they have gone forever. Certainly the mackerel which once crowded the waters off the south-west coast are less abundant, having been decimated by commercial fishermen using nets as large as St Paul's Cathedral, and by careless foreign trawlers. But other fish are also scarcer than they were. The satisfactions which Derek and I experienced are still there, but the variety and weight of catches are not: only the very lucky can hope to find in a week what we commonly found in a day.

Or even, in a night, for we also fished from the pier after dark, drawing strange comfort from the twinkling of the harbour lights and the lapping of the sea against the piles. It was exciting not to know what was happening at the end of one's line, and we only detected bites by means of a bell, attached to the line with a clothes peg. One or two rings probably meant a pouting: repeated jangling, like the bells of a Morris dancer, usually signified the arrival of a shoal of Channel whiting.

Some people, perhaps because of the tired and tasteless versions they were forced to eat at school, take a jaundiced view of whiting. Served fresh, however, it is firm-fleshed and delicious. One fellow-angler, a regular on the pier, would catch one, gut it, pop it into a bucket of boiling water (kept hot over a spirit stove) and eat it straight from the bone, all in the space of a few minutes. That way, as he generously allowed us to find out, a whiting would satisfy the most demanding palate.

Derek's grandparents were careful but liberal guardians. I suppose because they knew we went fishing rather than looking for mischief, they gave us free rein. Thus after the night-fishing, when we became more adventurous and moved along the coast to the mini-fiords beyond Seahaven, they put no barriers in our way.

We went there for wrasse, a fish with a very extended family, like a Scottish clan which takes in a wide variety of different types. There are more than 400 species of wrasse in the world, ranging in size from a few inches to some, not seen in British waters, over thirty feet. Most of them are found in the tropics: almost all are very pretty.

The ballan and the occasional cuckoo wrasse for which we fished have never been commercially important in Britain, but they do make good eating, despite their spikes. What made them attractive to us was simply their dazzling appearance and the way they seemed to change colour in the water. They were all greens and blues, with yellow and orange rings round their dorsal fins. They would have looked more at home among the corals of the Pacific than in the rock gullies of Sussex.

Mostly we enjoyed them for the sport they gave us, and then, having admired their beauty, we returned them to the sea. We did the same, for we were now incipient conservationists, with the garfish we caught. But I confess that the temptation to keep garfish was not strong. Unlike wrasse, garfish are never a sweet sight: even after cooking them, their bones still manage to convey displeasure by turning a bright and off-putting green.

One of their alternative names is sea-pike, presumably because they are longish and snake-like, with a baleful eye, and with nasty bony snouts which make them hard to hook. We sought them out with our boys' tackle using a freshwater float and a sliver of mackerel as bait, casting about fifteen yards out to the shoal and hitting them immediately the float disappeared. As soon as they were hooked they would leap aerobatically and then run up and down furiously in the water. They fought well, and we respected them, but they were not fish to write poems about.

All these different fish and all this fishing could have sickened us of the sport, but they did not. Although we later went different ways, Derek and I have continued to take pleasure in our absorbing art. Those days and nights at Newhaven gave us a unique grounding in every branch of angling, and because we were largely self-taught, from watching and listening to practical experts, our knowledge stuck. Few schoolboys now have access to as many different natural fishing places as we did, and some will never have fished anywhere except on an artificially stocked lake.

Perhaps my memories of our idyll are tinged with more than a little roseate imaginings: perhaps not all our days were fun. We can hardly have endured all our disappointments without occasional discontents, and we must, at times, have yearned to be with other children in a warm cinema rather than standing on some exposed rock.

But if we did, I choose not to remember. I view those halcyon days with affection. We learned all kinds of things at Newhaven, and when Derek's grandfather died, and his grandmother had to give up her house, we knew that we would never again enjoy anything in quite the same innocent way. I was grateful for being able to escape the suburban blight of St Paul's Cray. I was grateful for the friendship of the Maw family and for the tolerance with which my own parents had let me reach out to wider horizons. Altogether, and notwithstanding that I didn't live in one of the Tudor farmhouses I went past in the train, I had been very lucky.

If I envied anyone, it was only the imaginary son whom the imaginary Mr Crabtree, who figured in a *Daily Mirror* cartoon strip of the time, took out on fishing lessons. Three years after Newhaven, I met Mr Crabtree's creator. He was Bernard Venables, a legendary figure in the angling world, who worked on *Creel*, the most lavish fishing magazine ever produced. When I submitted an illustration to him for publication and had it accepted, I could hardly believe my good fortune. I had long admired his articles and fishing paintings, and when he put his seal of approval on my work, my cup ran over. I knew then that art as well as fishing would be my life.

3

Seaside and Sunfish

Even in the months before Derek's grandfather died, he and I had moved away from the gentle exploration of ponds and streams to uncover the mysteries of sea-fishing. Wilful Channel breakers crashing into rocky gullies and onto shingle beaches offered us greater excitements than the placid waters of the sleepy villages inland. Our targets were now bass and mullet rather than perch and roach: we welcomed the sea's inconstancy, the spray in our faces and the sense of the vastness of the oceans beyond our tiny reach. Subconsciously, perhaps, we were looking to a wider world beyond Denton. We were beginning to recognise, even if we could not define, new longings and ambitions.

Perhaps we recognised, too, that the high tide of our fishing friendship had begun, almost imperceptibly, to ebb. Although I was still to fish occasionally with Derek elsewhere, we never went back to Newhaven together. I became more solitary and introspective, spending most weekends alone and loitering on rocks and beaches, a fishing squire seeking his spurs and contemplating, perhaps rather sentimentally, the nature of the world and the place I would have in it.

On one occasion, I took the train to Hastings and fished solidly for four days and nights, entirely alone. It was a revealing experience. At two o'clock on the last morning, I hooked a fish which, in earlier days, I would have risked life and limb to land. To my surprise, I found myself regarding it as just another fish. I couldn't see it without peering over the edge of the rocks, but I could feel it, and it was huge. And yet I lost it without pain, undisturbed by the knowledge that I had let myself miss something very special. During my lonely sojourn on the cold rocks, I had begun to discover, as Izaak Walton and others had discovered before me, that fishing teaches one more than how to catch fish.

I had indeed taken a few whiting and pouting and an occasional conger eel. But I had also, and unwittingly, caught something else less tangible; a sense of

...something far more deeply interfused,
Whose dwelling is in the light of setting suns,
And the round ocean and the living air.

Wordsworth and I may not have been thinking of exactly the same things, but I knew what he meant. My fishing was bringing me closer to the heart of things: with the egotism common to all adolescents, I thought I could hold eternity in the palm of the same hand which held my rod and line. I felt I was on the euphoric verge of discovering the secret of the universe.

Since then, along with everyone else, I have learned that wisdom does not arrive overnight, like a pools win. It has to be sought, and garnered in penny packets, over many years. Experience in itself has no value unless it is mulled over and digested, and so, like most artists and fishermen, I still take time out alone, as I did in my youth, to contemplate and to draw strength and inspiration from nature.

But I am no eremite. I like being in a sociable crowd as much as I like being on an empty river-bank. Thus when I bought myself a beach casting rod, and joined the cheery weekend company of sea-anglers who night-fished for winter cod from Deal pier, I enjoyed the banter and the good humour of like-minded madmen, which is what many people, with some reason, thought we were.

Pintail drake, the most attractive of ducks

The tackle shop near the sea stayed open late, ready to serve the last-minute needs of people coming down on the Friday night trains from London, and to distribute their pre-ordered bait. There would then be a rush to seek the best places on the pier, to get ready the hissing Tilley lamps, and to tie on bait and hooks. This was not easy, for Kentish winters can be savage. The winds used to tear in from the North Sea in demented, icy blasts, bringing flurries of biting hail in their wake. Fingers fumbled and froze. Swathed in layers of thick clothing, like Siberian peasants, men waited for the cod with a patience which few of them, I would guess, would display in other circumstances.

'The worse the weather, the better the cod,' they used to say, and no doubt they were right. But finding out the truth of this maxim for yourself demanded warm blood and much grit, for even when the official temperature was not too low, the chill factor struck deeply. What brought people to this bleak sport, I wondered, and what brought *me* to it?

Perhaps it was the exhilaration to be gained from battling with, and winning against, the elements. Perhaps it was simply the warmth of the camaraderie which builds up between people sharing joint ardours. And perhaps, in my case, it was the feeling of belonging to an exclusive club, populated largely by minor eccentrics. Sea-fishermen were, and are, a special breed of men: more social, possibly, than inland anglers, and more inclined to foregather in groups. They tend to know each other, and to meet during the week as well as at weekends. They revel in wind and bad weather: they joke a lot, and drink, and the London ones used to descend on the Kentish sea-ports like amiable, off-duty Vikings, intent on pleasure rather than pillage. Yet they were kind to young newcomers, and I remember with much affection many weekends spent in their boisterous company.

By now, I had left school to work as a junior in a London art-studio which supplied photographic and sketch-design material to the advertising industry. Derek had gone on to art-school, and I was never sure whether or not to envy him. At least I was being paid, and the talented professionals with whom I worked could teach me as much as any lecturers. They operated in a very competitive industry, and had to be good to survive: the grounding I got from them in air-brushing, re-touching and other techniques was as thorough as any I could have been given anywhere.

Emboldened by my work experience, I was now beginning to take my drawing seriously, and to submit sketches to various magazines. At the same time, I was learning more and more about fishing. When, as the office junior, I had to make special deliveries of finished art work to our advertising customers, mostly in the West End and the City, I had plenty of chances to browse through up-market tackle shops. I spent many stolen moments lustfully viewing rods and tackle far beyond my financial reach. Eventually, obsessed with the thought of working amidst such treasure, I got a job in Gamages' tackle department, 'on contingency'. This was hardly a sound basis for a rewarding, upwardly-progressing future, but it suited me: four pounds ten shillings a week, and plenty of time to handle the best rods and inspect the best tackle. I developed then the love of well-made fishing equipment which has never left me since.

Fishing and sketching absorbed all of my leisure time. My box-like bedroom in St Paul's Cray was stuffed with pieces of tackle and bursting with embryo sketches. I became a proud and happy member of the Tonbridge and District Angling Club and continued, when not fishing with them in the Medway, to pursue my sea-fishing off the Kentish coast.

Mostly, I still went after the cod which came down the East Coast from the far north. Perhaps I was intrigued by the chance of making an outside catch, for then, if not now, cod came both in abundance and in sizes to delight the most ambitious specimen hunter. Twenty-pounders were common.

Sometimes, eschewing the familiarities of Deal, I would seek out Derek and go with him to the shingle beaches of Dungeness. Here, we happily probed the richness of an offshore gully to the north-east of the old lighthouse known as The Dustbin*. This gully was formed by eddying tides between the boundaries of the shingle and the sand, and it was usually full of feed — slipper limpets, shrimp, hermit crabs, immature flatfish and the like — which used to wash back and forth in tempting dance for days after the gales dumped it there.

We used longbow casting rods with various reels, one of which was American, the Penn Beachmaster, with a lightweight, plastic spool which could revolve very fast. As brakes, we employed our youthful thumbs, searing them with the friction's heat, and disregarding the pain for the sake of our art. We had to cast a hundred yards or more, which was less easy then than it is with today's lightweight and much improved tackle.

Sometimes, the spool would keep revolving after the lead had landed and the line would go into a fearsome 'bird's nest' which took an hour or more to untangle. Our fingers grew numb and

---

*Anyone wishing to unravel the phenomenon of The Dustbin should refer to an article by Leslie Moncrieff in the now defunct *Creel* Magazine for July 1963, pp.33-4, entitled 'The Fishing of Dungeness'.

ceased to work: the bird's nest was usually abandoned. We used to cut our losses and make good from the thousand yards of spare line we carried with us as a matter of routine. It was a rocky road to pleasure, but no one had forced us to travel along it: the hardships were part of the fun.

Leslie Moncrieff was the expert on cod and how to fish for it. He frequently caught twenty-pounders off Dungeness and then generously, through *Creel* magazine, told all the rest of us how to do the same. He developed a particular 'laid back' method of casting which almost everyone adopted, and his name was revered among the devotees of a sport which, for some of its practitioners, was almost a religion. Unlike trout men, or specialists in carp or barbel or all the rest, some of whom have been known to spend time with their wives and families, the dedication of those Kentish sea-fishermen was total: gales, hailstorms, rain, sleet — nothing diverted them from their chosen paths.

Fishing for cod from hire boats also drew large numbers from offices in the City. From time to time I went out with some of these high-spirited sportsmen, usually in a group of eight or ten, under an experienced and sardonic skipper. We would set out in good order, but it was rarely long before the heaving sea took its cruel toll. More than half the party would come back green and limp, having spent most of the trip retching over the gunnels of the small work boat. Returning in the train from such expeditions, little relishing the smell of fish and sea-sick, which must have lingered in the carriage for days afterwards, I sometimes wondered heretically why some of my fellow-travellers did not take up some other sport.

Cod was not my only quarry, nor did I fish exclusively from Deal. Once, seeking to escape the adult company of the hire-boat parties, I arranged to go to Herne Bay with my younger brother. I was just over fifteen and he was eleven. Under my fraternal guidance, he would catch skate from the pier, at night.

Unhappily, I failed to do my homework. When we arrived off the train from St Mary Cray, where I had picked him up, it was blowing hard. We staggered to the pier under the burden of our extensive gear with little enthusiasm on his part. 'You'll enjoy it,' I said, but even I had misgivings. The early autumn night showed no signs of being a balmy one: indeed, it was cold and wet and getting colder.

We reached the pier. It was closed for night-fishing, and the re-opening time next spring seemed rather far away. Forlornly, and not with much conviction, I sought a suitable promontory instead of the deserted pier, but the night was raw and my brother was crying with the cold. It was clear that his joy in my sport was less than unconfined. I recognised defeat: wet, weary, cold and hungry, we took the train home, and it was a long time before my brother ever fished again.

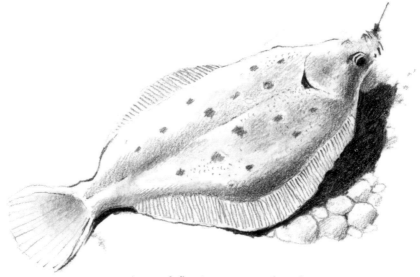

A good flattie comes to beach

That was my worst fishing night ever, for I had desperately wanted to communicate my own enthusiasms to a willing sibling, and I had failed. But I still continued to make sporadic excursions with Derek, and we enjoyed several instructional trips with Ron Edwards, a tackle dealer with some reputation as a specimen skate hunter, to unravel the mysteries of the Goodwin Sands. Here Ron taught us to find the gullies full of young mussels which attracted flatfish, and how to fish for the plaice and flounders which abounded there.

All of these seaside outings were grist to my fishing mill. I enjoyed them and they taught me new skills. I became so addicted to sea-fishing that I kept my clothes and gear in the office so that, on Fridays, I could get straightaway to my chosen weekend location without wasting a minute. One night, rushing into the station waiting-room at Deal to change, I found out that my brothers in commercial art, knowing my plans, had sewn up every hole that could be sewn up in my jacket and trousers. They had also substituted cotton wool for the cheese in my sand-wiches. It was par for the office course; of a piece with their sending me out, when I first worked there, for a box of dots or a tube of Veronica Lake. Anyone with the kind of obsession I had for angling was fair game, but their ribbing was always punctuated with kindnesses and they were broadminded enough to respect my youthful enthusiasms.

After Finsbury Park and the Darent; after the Denton hammer-ponds and the Sussex coast; after the cold chase for cod off Deal and Dungeness, and the less robust search for Goodwins' flatfish, I was ceasing to be an apprentice and beginning to acquire the status of journeyman, if not quite that of master fisherman. When Derek and I went back to Sussex to fish for bass, we were no longer innocents. We went looking for specimens, not the run-of-the-mill creatures we had been content to catch off Newhaven pier.

This time, we fished the little fiords indenting the coastline below the downs where the bass tended to feed. It needed skill to land a bait without getting it on the rocks or the abounding kelp. To make things more difficult, we at first used hardback crabs as bait. Then, in the end, moved by failure, we shifted to 'peelers' – crabs which are just about to slough their shells to reveal the membrane of a new shell beneath the old. Take the shell off a 'hardback' which is not in the process of changing, and you simply have a gooey mess which, for reasons unknown, have no appeal for the big bass we sought.

These fish were great sport on light tackle, and the bigger ones, six or seven pounds and upwards, could fight as well as any leaping salmon. Now, their nursery areas in the estuaries have become less habitable, through pollution, and this, combined with the overfishing of schools of bass by drift net, has much reduced the population. Legislation prohibiting the taking of the species below a certain size does exist, but is not always followed: bass is too good to eat for some restaurants to query any that they are dubiously offered.

Rock- and shore-fishing offer the same freedoms as fishing a Dartmoor stream, and the same opportunities to commune with wild nature. Britain has some 6000 miles of coastline and all of it, give or take a defence establishment or two, is open to anyone who wants to enjoy it. The lonelier rocks and foreshores have the same mystique as the upper moors: you can still walk there, or sit fishing from a rocky outcrop, with no more than the sea-birds and the sound of the waves to disturb your thoughts.

Sea-fishing is heterogeneous: it provides an infinite variety of catches. Going for one thing, you are often just as likely to strike another. Sometimes the unexpected will be welcome, and sometimes not, but everything will be of interest. The mundane and the exotic share a common element: even in the grey wastes of the North Sea, strange fish can appear, far from their normal haunts.

Once, chatting to a pier fisherman in Deal, the bell on the end of his rod jangled violently. He struck, hooked what looked like a mass of seaweed, and after a long struggle landed a sun-fish; a rare sight around our coasts, but a pretty one. Catching such a creature adds spice to fishing life: it conjures visions of olives and rough wine, and old, stone houses straggling down, under a hot sun, to seas bluer than our own.

Even off the Kent coast, where it is hard to imagine that the slate-grey sea has anything left to yield into the hands of city-dwellers who ravage it from boats and shore, one can still catch uncommon fish, such as the lumpsucker and the weaver. But it is more by chance than design, and you must be cautious in handling them. For the weaver carries a poison, in a small sac beneath its dorsal fin, which can be lethal. Grab it, or some others of these rare species, without care and you could be badly stung; although if you can remove its venom safely, then the Greater Weaver makes superb eating.

So many different fish in so many southeastern places: the appetite was beginning to sicken a little, though not to die completely. But other interests, not previously acknowledged during my single-minded pursuit of fishing perfection, had sneakily begun to intrude upon my puritan consciousness. I began to hear the sound of the Beatles, and notice clothes, and see girls. The call of the wild, winter beaches was becoming drowned by the insistent throbbing which emerged, temptingly, from Saturday-night discos. I was beginning, in short, to be overcome by forces over which most of us have little control. I was learning that even fishermen have weaknesses.

Since those days, my sea-fishing has been relatively limited to outings on the Mull of Kintyre and the Devon coasts. On the Mull, I fished for pollack as though spinning for sea-trout, although at a greater depth. Using a large, heavy toby or a German sprat as lures, I used to cast out as far as I could, gauging the depth of the kelp beds and bringing the bait across the top of them. It was exciting and dangerous, since the water, even close in to the rocks, was fifteen or twenty fathoms deep and the tides were strong: it was as well to be confident in your swimming, and sure-footed in your movements over the rocks, before you embarked on the pursuit.

With the right sky, the waters of the Mull could be beautifully clear. As I looked down on one occasion, a big pollack darted into sight then shied away. I saw why. Behind it was a huge basking shark, filtering plankton through its great gill rakers, its dorsal fin every so often breaking the surface of the blue water with all the menace of a Jaws. I had seen such sharks before, but never as close as five or six yards away. The nearness of this one filled me with both awe and alarm. But I also felt a strange sense of peace, for even though this was a fish, it had the same aura as the gentle whale, a mammal. Perhaps the tranquil atmosphere of the Mull transfers itself to all around it: after the busy south of England, it is a haven for naturalists and fishermen of every sort.

I think I shall probably continue to climb Bengullion, the hill behind Campbeltown, until I no longer have the breath, just to look down on the bays and beaches which provide such splendid sea-fishing. And I shall continue to roam the coast there with a sketch-book and a light rod, much as I do on Dartmoor. But whether I shall ever go back to the serious winter cod-fishing off Deal, which occupied much of my earlier years, I strongly doubt. That kind of sport is best left, perhaps, to hardier souls than mine. The high tides of that era have gone, and I am now content with less ambitious catches.

Yet what do they know of fishing who only know placid ponds and quiet lakes? I'm very glad that I sea-fished, and very lucky that I shall continue to have the chance, on the uncrowded Mull, to seek all the varieties of fish which, sadly, are no longer quite so common off Sussex and Kent. Perhaps some day governments will return to sense and adopt policies which strike a fair balance between commerce and conservation. For so long as there are seaside holidays, and rocks, and piers, children of all ages will want to fish from them. Will there always be something for them to catch?

4
Coarse Fish and Fine Specimens

In September 1952, Richard Walker caught the largest carp ever to be taken with rod and line in Britain. It weighed forty-four pounds, about the size of a small goat, and lived on for many years after its capture in London Zoo, under the name of Clarissa.

The taking of Clarissa confirmed Walker's position as one of the leading innovative fishermen in the country. It also marked the beginning of the esoteric cult of 'specimen hunting', a manic pursuit which seems to live, and die, and live again in small numbers of anglers in every new generation.

Walker extolled the delights of catching big fish in a book called *No Need To Lie*. He and various friends such as Jack Hargreaves, Denys Watkins-Pytchford, John Norman and a few others, founded The Carp Catchers' Club and began to revolutionise the way many people looked at fishing. They were no longer content to sit beside a quiet pond or stream and catch fish, or simply enjoy the countryside. They wanted to catch the biggest fish, the 'specimens', and in doing so, they set themselves

Cod fishing, Dungeness

Robin Armstrong '87

apart from the common run of amiable and relatively disorganised men who fished for fun, happy with a day out under the sun and with whatever catch the gods offered them.

By the time the 'Swinging Sixties' arrived, a decade when

Snipe

every odd fancy was promoted to its limit, specimen hunting was well established. The new generation, of which I was one, took it up with zest and delight. We saw in it the angling equivalent of the mini-skirt; a new fad which flaunted convention and defied tradition.

In those wild years, style counted for more than substance. The medium was the message, and the soup can was more important than the soup. What you did mattered less than how you did it. And no hobby could retain its attraction for young people unless it afforded opportunities to 'turn on and tune in' to something new, different and preferably recondite. Specimen hunting fulfilled these criteria. And after the manner of the day, it even provided us with our own guru. Walker himself became our Piscine Maharishi, and we his self-important disciples. Our sport became almost a religion.

Walker's followers were men who took themselves seriously. They went for the big ones; the difficult ones; the ones which were hard to find. They travelled furtively, kept their destinations secret and moved in very mysterious ways their wonders to perform. They were men of few words, at least until they wrote up their successes, and they walked alone. Like latter-day Captain Scotts, they equipped themselves for every eventuality and sought assistance from no one.

Among fishermen, a specimen hunter, actual or fledgling, was not hard to spot. His general air of anxiety (were eight large loaves enough to provide groundbait for the day to come?); his stooped shoulders (weary with the burden of all his equipment); his puckered face (creased with the fear that someone might have found his secret patch); his special clothes (even the pattern of his camouflage jacket had to be right), and his gear (matching bite alarms, perhaps?), all marked him out from lesser breeds without the proper lore.

Other anglers may have been cheerful, gregarious fellows, like my sea-fishing friends: specimen hunters eschewed all company but their own circle. And yet, for reasons which I cannot now understand, we worshipped them. In the Sixties, they were what all keen young anglers aspired to be.

Perhaps it was simply that, in an age of a thousand false prophets, Walker had more claim to respect than most. He was a true innovator in tackle design and fishing methods and his book, *Still Water Angling**, was both readable and illuminating. We followed him with all the enthusiasm which that generation expended on anything defying an established pattern. We read his articles and books; we copied him where we could, and we envied his freedom to fish in places like Redmire Pool, in faraway Herefordshire, where he and his favoured cronies regularly caught their large carp.

I look back on that youthful self with a wry inner smile, not quite sure how I could have succumbed to the lure of a form of fishing which negated so much of my present philosophy. I don't believe, now, that fishing has to be about huge catches or big fish. My perceptions have changed. I have no objection to angling competitions, but if they become ends in themselves, my interest fades. I see fishing as very much more than a vying for first place and minor fame.

*R.Walker, *Still Water Angling* (MacGibbon & Kee: 1973).

But in those earlier days, I was intrigued by the glamour which seemed to surround those for whom specimen hunting was a way of life. I revelled in their exploits and tried hard to emulate them. I was carried away by the secrecy, the rituals, the exclusivity and the sheer snobbery of it all. It was a while before I began to see the whole curious business in any perspective.

The very essence of a specimen hunter was his equipment. Even though much of it was never used, he carried enough gear to survive a world war, or perhaps start one. And the more he carried, the greater the mystique which surrounded him. No one made rules about what could be worn or carried: you either knew instinctively what was right, in which case you were accepted into the charmed circle, or you did not, in which case you were despatched, metaphorically, into the non-members' stand. As with all English social and sporting worlds, conduct was governed by conventions which were nonetheless strict for not having been listed or explained. Many failed the entrance test without even knowing that they had been tested.

What the acceptable specimen hunter needed were:

Item, a pair of Richard Walker carp rods and a pair of Avons to go with them, together with rod rests and bite indicators;

Item, a Mitchell Fixed Spool Reel with either the original half bail arm, or the later one with a full bail arm, but positively not the high-speed variety;

Item, a large, 45-inch diameter umbrella, camouflaged and with all the metal parts painted matt black, to prevent reflections which might disturb the fish: one friend even painted the bail arm on his Mitchell reel lest it dazzle when he flicked it off;

Item, and an important one, since it displayed exaggerated optimism in one's own abilities, a landing net big enough to house a large shark;

Item, binoculars, being careful not to flash them in the sunshine during the day, and used for checking the progress of other specimen hunters who were probably using theirs to watch you;

Item, a reclining camp bed, on which to remain motionless or comatose (and frozen) for up to twenty-four hours;

Item, one primus stove, not actually essential to the catching of
the fish, but a nice piece of kit, which marked you out as
a long-distance man;

Item, barley sugar, to compensate for the food you never
cooked on your primus stove;

Item, one powerful torch which was taboo to operate except
during the day, to show that you had one, and

Item, two or three large, loose-weave hessian sacks, one to be
kept out for carrying your seven or eight loaves of bread,
and the others to hold any carp which you might attract.

I carried hessian sacks with me for years, but hardly ever used
them. I hardly ever used up my bread, either, but I went on
carrying too much of it for too long, simply because I thought it
would help advance my claim to senior status.

All of this impedimenta was quite difficult to hump about,
since few of us had motor cars in those days. On the other hand,
the trains were more accommodating then than now, and I rather
enjoyed the captive audience they afforded for my one-man
show. For dress was as important to a specimen hunter as his
equipment, and I liked to think I cut rather a dash.

The hat came first. It had to be a Walker-type trilby; floppy,
with no flies in the band, but plenty of brim (later, at least among
the young, the brim became narrower), well-used and rain-
soaked, and above all, worn with flair. Clothing had to be olive-
green or khaki drab, probably a safari jacket with lots of pockets:
the camouflage jacket came later. Shoes included plimsolls, so
that you could creep round the edge of your chosen lake, as much
to find out what your rivals were doing as to spot fish, and
waders, so that you could paddle a few inches into the water,
keeping the vegetation behind you.

We thought we looked pretty good; dedicated, purposeful, cool
and stylish. Lord Home might be fishing the Tweed much as his
grandfather might have done, and in much the same old suit, but
we were pace-setters; bringing in change; promoting the latest in
fishing fashion and making our own contribution to the Sixties'

revolution. Specimen hunting was the new thing and we were its standard-bearers: everything about our tackle and our clothes had to be right.

And yet, even with all the proper equipment and the approved dress, it was still possible to fall short of the accolade. No one ever quite knew what finally marked out the specimen hunter from the competent coarse fisherman or game fisherman, but everyone recognised the difference between them. What was the elusive quality which so many sought in vain to achieve?

I am not sure that I ever really knew. To gain recognition by the demi-gods who wrote for *Creel* and *Angling* magazines, you certainly had to have applied the whole of your being to the pursuit of big fish, and to have caught some, preferably under difficult circumstances. And you certainly had to be seen in the right fishing places. But after that, the matter remained obscure: I only know that many applied themselves to the quest for recognition, but few succeeded in getting it. Maybe we all tried too hard.

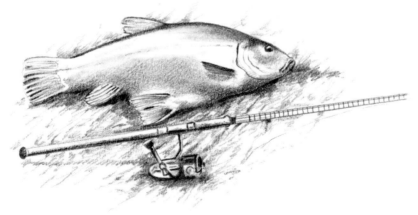

Specimen tench with Mk IV rod

Walker, in my view, was the most influential fishing personality since Izaak Walton. He was a fishing intellectual with a strong, practical sense, who was able both to argue his theories in print and to prove them conclusively on the water. He could fish successfully for anything from perch to salmon. The rod he designed for catching carp and pike (he also produced an equally good, lightened-down version for chub and tench) was ideally suited to its serious purpose: nowadays, it is highly prized by collectors throughout Britain.

Walker knew everything about fish and their environments. He knew that, to catch them, you had first to observe them and the water in which they moved. He knew about eddies and ripples and underhangs and the state of the river; he knew about lures and baits and weather conditions, and above all, he knew how to apply his knowledge. He was an all-round master of the angling arts, but never a solemn one, and I suspect that his strong sense of humour must often have led him to smile gently at the puritan excesses of his more extreme devotees. For them, pain and suffering were part of the religion: the more discomfort you endured, the greater became your claim to high-priestly status.

Winter night-fishing for carp, not then a common practice, exemplified this masochistic philosophy. Since carp rarely feed much between November and March, little is to be gained by fishing for them. But the myths of serious fishing had to be sustained: to be prepared to lie awake, cramped and stiff, to wait upon your bite alarm, betokened the kind of dedication which marked you out from the common run. Even if it brought you no great success, you could fairly claim to have honoured the Specimen Hunters' unwritten code of Uncomfortable Angling Practice. Your place in the Honours Roll would be properly assured, and you might even get a letter describing your tenebrous experiences published in *Creel* or *Angling*.

Creel and *Angling* were the two main fishing publications of the time. *Creel* in particular was lavishly produced and illustrated, but both had very expert fishermen working for them in all departments. Men like Ewan Clarkson; Jim Gibbinson; the late Terry Brown; Brian Harris; John Cooper; Tony Johnson; Trevor Housby and Peter Stone were all stars of the specimen-hunting world, with a vast range of fishing expertise. I knew of them through reading about them: sometimes I actually met them, in various London pubs and tackle shops, notably Peeks in Gray's Inn Road.

Tony Johnson became a good friend. When we decided on a trip to Norfolk, to extract what we hoped would be a monster pike from the East Anglian reed beds, we prepared ourselves like knights before battle. Not content with our twelve herrings and four pounds of sprats and various wobbling spoons, we decided we must have live bait. We sought it in Broadlands, a lake in Kent. Unhappily, we had both become so engrossed in our pursuit of big fish that we had almost lost the art of catching the small ones. It took us longer than we anticipated to get half-a-dozen perch and a few roach into the bucket we proposed to use for transporting them.

We set out for Norfolk the following morning in a wet but warm dawn. The canvas bucket containing our live bait was no substitute for a proper can, but it was the only piece of our extensive gear which was not pukka. We had four rods apiece (what grim harvest had we in view, I wonder?), plus reels, carp nets, sprats, and a biblical number of large, dead herring to go with our live fish. As always, we were equipped for every eventuality.

Tony's car, a Wolsey Hornet, was a refined version of a Mini, but no bigger. On a warm, humid day, with two largish men in it, together with all their fishing impedimenta, it was cramped and uncomfortable. I worried about the live bait lest it become one with the herrings and sprats before we got to our appointed killing grounds. The smell of fish in the small car was overpowering, but we couldn't open the windows because of the rain.

Stooping, I waggled my finger in the water of the canvas bucket in vigorous circles, a one-man oxygenating machine trying to keep the live bait on this side of the Great Divide. I cannot say how my charges felt about the journey, but I found it very disagreeable. They, at least, were cool and relatively free to move about. I was not. Even now, I can still see the crease in my torso where I bent over, for several hours, to perform my watery version of the kiss of life.

We reached Norfolk intact. We fished hard, but we caught nothing. The four rods apiece; the reels; the carp nets; the live bait; the dead bait and the wobbling spoons availed us not. It was a typical specimen hunter's day out, full of discomfort, high endeavour and no pike. And yet, at the time, I enjoyed it, or thought I did, although what I probably enjoyed was talking about it afterwards and recounting the technical details of our frustrating day. Suffice it to say that I should not like to repeat the experience, unless Tony now has a very large, air-conditioned car, with an ice-box in the boot for the dead fish and somewhere to put the rods where they couldn't poke me in the eye.

There were other days, and other journeyings. 'B.B.' (a pseudonym used by Denys Watkins-Pytchford) was now beginning to give hints about the places favoured by him and his colleagues which they had previously kept secret. Specimen hunting was becoming more popular, while the criteria for acceptance into the ranks of its practitioners were becoming less rigorous. In 1966, the hallowed waters of Redmire Pool were opened to people other than the members of the Carp Catchers' Club. Carp-fishing boomed.

There had been good reasons, not just a desire for exclusivity, for the previous restrictions on Redmire. Various experiments and observations had been made there, which a free-for-all would have rendered impossible. But the opening of Redmire served as a symbol. I, along with almost every other coarse fisherman, was swept up in the fashion for chasing large carp.

The layman, half-remembering stories about sleek monks and well-stocked monastery carp ponds, might think such fishing tame and undemanding. It is not: rather, it offers fine sport. I enjoyed 'crust fishing', using either crusts or soft pellets of bread; and creeping round the edge of the lake in plimsolls, observing the fish to determine where it was going and getting there before it. Then, and carefully, I would lay my decoy crusts and plant my casts from lily-pad to lily-pad. I enjoyed it because it was a very visual way to fish: to see a large carp come up to take the crust, greedily and indelicately, and hear the indrawn 'kloop' as he sucked it down in one huge gulp, like a giant vacuum cleaner, is one of the most exciting of angling's many rewards. And then to watch him rush off to the safety of the deep, knowing that you may have hooked your monster fish, crowns your pleasure. No one could claim that carp-fishing is dull.

The Walker carp rod has a soft action tip so that, when one casts, a soft bait like bread crust will not come adrift from the hook. To use it is rather like fishing for brown trout with a big, bushy, dry fly, and requires the same accuracy of casting to put the crust down on one's chosen lily pad, or just behind it. I never thought it easy.

I mostly use bread as bait, but the true carp men employ more esoteric temptations. Kevin Maddocks* records the use of sultanas, maggots, sweetcorn, kidney beans, cod roes, luncheon meat, cockles, hemp, maple high protein (a kind of pea), red dari seeds, spearmint, spam and tiger nuts. And something called Duncan Kay's Red Slyme.

Like medieval apothecaries seeking the elixir of life, carp men try anything and everything in their search for the right stuff. One carefully calculated formula was six ounces of calcium caseinate, together with two ounces each of baby milk, semolina and sugar-bread, with breadcrumbs from the freshest, best-quality brown bread. No convention of master chefs could have taken more care over their concoctions than the specimen hunters.

One man took with him, to Redmire Pool, twenty boxes of cat food, of which he spread six on the water as soon as he arrived. Each box contained 500 morsels. Another took 70 lbs of iced shrimps, almost enough protein to keep an orphanage of starving children in good health for a month. And what of the ten packets of different-coloured jelly tots distributed by the same man on another occasion?

If carp could speak, they would have many tales to tell of sumptuous free banquets and crazy feasts — perhaps beginning with black pudding and ending with Black Magic. But I suppose there is little distinction between the carp man and his obsession with baits, and the trout man with his thousands of flies. The difference is not one in kind, but merely in degree: all fishermen are slightly mad, but some are madder than others.

*See K.Clifford & L.Arberry, *Redmire Pool*, Beekay Publishers, 1985, pp.143–73.

Big carp are hard to catch because big carp are old carp, which have been growing ever fatter for perhaps eighteen years or so. And no fish survives for that length of time in a weed-filled pool unless it has acquired much cunning and a good nose for potential danger. If it takes tiger nuts or kidney beans to lure such a fish out of its murky fastness, then so be it. And if you have discovered some even more effective enticement, then

R.A. with a Crafthole carp — I caught it eleven times in 1984

perhaps it is not unnatural, considering your investment of time and energy, that you would want to keep your formula secret from the man on the other bank. The specimen hunters were reticent to the point of paranoia about everything except their successes: they remained silent about their baits and their methods even amongst members of different rotas on the same pool.

At the same time, they were totally dedicated. Dick Walker caught five carp at Redmire Pool in 460 hours of fishing in 1952: in 1987, Kevin Maddocks, showing the same application, expects to spend at least seventy nights in his search for the one to break all records.

Apart from his carp rod, all Richard Walker's designs for fishing tackle reflected his engineering background. For the perch of Arlsley Lake, where crowds of small feeding perch on the surface made it difficult to reach the bigger fish beneath, he produced a special weight (popularly known as the Arlsley Bomb) to go with his long rod and fixed spool reel. It was a heavy and aerodynamically correct lead, with one end pointed, and a swivel at the other to ensure that it would not kink: a typical Walker innovation, simple, practical and highly successful. I still use mine a great deal.

I also continue to use the Richard Walker reservoir rod, a Superlite, made by Hardy Brothers; it is still the best ever produced, even if, because of new materials, it has now become slightly outdated. It has good length, a good feel and enough body and substance to take a large sea-trout. When I fail to catch anything with it, I know that I must blame myself, not my tackle.

Sadly, Dick Walker died a year or so ago but he is well remembered and hugely admired. In the sporting jargon of today, he was a fisherman's fisherman: thoughtful, experienced and skilled, with the right angling instincts and a fine ability to communicate his ideas and his enthusiasms in very readable prose. When he began fishing 'put and take' venues, it was jokingly said that 'the big ones had been put in the day before'. But nobody seriously believed that. Walker could have found fish anywhere, and everyone knew it. Quite simply, he was the best angler of his time.

That period also bred other fishermen of distinction, and the magazines were full of articles written by good practical anglers who also knew the theory and wrote well about it. John Nixon, who took over from Bernard Venables as editor of *Creel*, and

Brian Harris, editor of *Angling*, were only two whose work fired my youthful enthusiasms. I knew, and much admired, both men, and when Harris once suggested a frivolous exercise with Terry Brown, John Cooper and Keith Linsell, I joined in the preparations very willingly.

The object was to prepare an illustrated article on the start of the coarse-fishing season, which opened at a minute past midnight on 16 June. We were to begin fishing then, carry on all night and write about what happened.

In the manner of our generation, we made huge preparations, baiting the lake near Terry's home until we could barely see the water, and borrowing all the best gear, including hand-made rods, from Keith, who worked in Peek's tackle shop. Our hopes were high. They grew even higher after several hours of pre-fishing drinks in Terry's local. By the time we began to fish, we were tipsily confident that nothing aquatic would survive the night.

We were very wrong. Whatever was in the pond, stayed in the pond. After fishing, and fishing, and fishing again, we caught nothing: perhaps all living creatures had been overcome by our combined breaths. Next morning, we left the pond as we found it. We were wiser, though heavy-headed.

In those days, of course, not many waters were actually stocked with carp. A very few had endemic populations of large fish, but they were neither as extensively publicised nor as extensively fished as they would be now, and their inhabitants were both sagacious and very wary of strange intrusions. Today, many ponds are carefully stocked, and good-sized carp are not so hard to catch. At one place in Devon, where I fish, I have taken the same fish about a dozen times, recognising it by its deformed backbone and the marks in its mouth. Indeed, over the past year, I have watched it grow from eleven to fourteen pounds.

Perhaps the old days always seem best, although all experience suggests that they are not. Anglers then had to find their own happy hunting waters without much help, relying mainly on word-of-mouth recommendations from friends. And when they got to their chosen fishing grounds, they had to pit their skills against natural fish instinctively schooled in the ways of survival. These were harder to catch than the stocked variety of today, although I never discount the ability of farmed fish, under constant attack from many eager rods, to avoid the hooks of day-permit holders, bearing gifts.

Pike fishing

Carp and pike were not the only acceptable quarry for specimen hunters. Apart from menials like gudgeon, any fish could be accounted a specimen provided it was outstanding of its type. Thus in one early phase of my specimen hunting, I fished for chub, on the Medway, relying for bait on luncheon meat supplied by an indulgent mother who thought me 'very wasteful'.

I had been attracted to what Izaak Walton called this 'fearfullest of fishes', ever ready to 'sink down towards the bottom of the water at the first shadow of your rod', by an experience on the Darent. Alone, bored and rather wet, I had taken shelter beneath a willow, and moodily begun to pass my heavy time by watching a fat slug inch along a damp leaf. I was just reflecting that my life was about as exciting as his when suddenly a spurt of rain washed him off the leaf and into the water.

Almost before I had had time to register what had happened,

the great wide mouth of a four-pound chub appeared and sucked him down. Fascinated, I found another slug and dropped that into the water. The same thing happened again.

Remembering Walton's warning about the chub's tremulousness, I gently and quietly took off the hook and float from my rod and replaced them with a single hook and another slug. Carefully, I let down the line. Within the instant, he had taken me into the weed bank: at the same time, his grace and pace converted me on the spot into a fisher of specimen chub.

But although I tried very hard, I never actually succeeded in taking a really big one. They were too clever for me: in theory, chub take anything terrestrial that looks as though it ought not to be there, but in practice they are more discriminating. The very fact that the big ones survive to a decent size means that they are chub from the 'A' stream: intelligent scholarship candidates who have no difficulty in recognising the traps set by sharp examiners for the unwary. Whatever tricks I tried, like casting crust onto a weed bed and letting it float off without a ripple, the real monsters — which I knew to be there — always eluded me. All I ever caught were of the size which fails to win the gold cups.

The carp, says my Walton, is 'a stately, a good, and a very subtle fish'; a description which hardly fits that of something which qualifies as 'coarse'. For 'coarse', in my dictionary, means ordinary or common; of inferior quality; wanting in delicacy of texture; and a carp is none of these things. But then neither are other coarse fish, nor coarse fishermen.

Coarse fish and coarse-fishing are perhaps unfair terms, and newcomers to fishing must not be put off by them: the beauty of different fish lies in the eyes of different fishermen. I do little coarse-fishing nowadays, but I have had as much pleasure in the past from catching carp as I have had from fishing for trout or mullet. For fishing is fishing is fishing, and all aspects of the sport merit respect. Only the cult of specimen hunting causes me to raise a mild, middle-aged eyebrow, and I confess to some gladness that I am no longer subject to its attendant rituals and absurdities.

5

Cherrybrook and Treacle Parkin

Fishing the inconstant streams of upland Dartmoor is not for those who measure their happiness in numbers and weight of fish taken. On rivers such as the East and West Dart, the Cherrybrook and the Cowsic, even the expert is rarely rewarded with a full bag. For most people, an outing will end with a catch of no more than a few small brownies, none of them stretching the scales much over a pound.

But they will be fish to delight the senses: firm-bodied, sparkling, exquisitely graceful; each one with a different and highly individual pattern of subtle brown and red speckles on a shining skin, and all of them precisely adapted to the untamed waters in which they spend their days. I marvel that even prodigal nature can lavish such wealth of careful beauty on anything so small, and question whether I, or any other painter, will ever totally succeed in capturing the living essence of such creatures in mere watercolour. I view them with wonder and occasionally, I confess, with the guilt which touches all hunters at one time or another. To see my respected quarry lying lifeless on the river-bank does not always fill me with unconfined joy.

Often, of course, I fish hard and take nothing. My cunning opponent outwits and eludes me; honours end evenly, and my efforts come to nought. Yet if I have been on Dartmoor all day, I shall have enjoyed myself, despite my apparent lack of success. *Piscator non solum piscatur*, says the motto of the Flyfishers' Club; there is more to fishing than fish. I will have seen the shadows of wild clouds racing across the hillsides; I will have felt the warmth which comes from exchanging greetings with trusted friends, and seen 'heaven in a wild flower'. Catch or no catch, my day will have been well spent, in country of infinite variety.

Buzzard, my favourite bird in the West country

Dartmoor's boundaries encompass valleys which are almost gentle and hills which are certainly harsh. The views, the light and the weather can change almost from hour to hour. Sunshine goes suddenly, as dark, heavy cumulus clouds race in from the south-west: mist falls, and the curlew goes silent. No more than half a mile from the road, and without a compass, it is easy to lose one's way: wise men follow the streams, and stay away from short cuts. In the damp, grey envelope which enfolds you, noises are stilled and the rest of the living world can seem very far away.

Tribute to R.W.

Robin Armstrong '87

Carp

head study of old brown trout
from the cherrybrooke, I always think of
the rather quaint description given to this
type of fish in Travis Jenkins "Fishes of the British Isles"
it reads "Old male trout with hook." Robin Armstrong '87

Some rare old tackle – The Compleat Angler

Beyond the motorway and the new town, primaeval England lurks unchanged.

Fishing on Dartmoor is real fishing. The rivers and streams are full of secret pools and lairs known only to the trout themselves and to the most experienced students of their vagrant ways. People like Harry Price, who sailed the world with the Royal Navy before settling down to make beautiful wooden carvings of his best catches; Phil Seppings, who could even teach Taff Price* about flies, and Annie Monro, who lives in splendid isolation near the Cherrybrook, knew every boulder in their chosen rivers, and every quirk of the fast rising and falling waters from which they took their sport. It would be an impertinence for a stranger to hope to know Dartmoor overnight.

These ancient streams were weathered out over thousands of years: they demand respect. You cannot cast and hope to pull out a fat three-pounder, hand-reared and sleek, as you might from

I would be happy to use no other flies when fishing than these three: l-r, Half Stone, Treacle Parkin, Tups Indispensable

some lake, artificially fashioned by the blade of a bulldozer. The fish in my rivers cannot be spooned out like croutons from soup: they have to be fished with guile, patiently wooed.

Fishermen in the South-West must walk their chosen streams

S.D.Price, author of *Rough Stream and Trout Flies*, A. & C. Black Ltd., London.

carefully and work for their successes. They are the Light Infantry of Fishermen, mobile and unaccoutred: stout boots, waterproof clothing, a light cane rod not more than six or seven feet (a seven-foot Hardy C.C.de France is perfect), a small bag and possibly a hand net are all they need for the pursuit. Plus, of course, the tenacity to clamber over rocks and tramp the muddied paths beside rivers which may be narrow, but which are often very hard to cross. For flies, my own favourites are Half Stone, a versatile fly which can be taken as 'anything the trout want it to be' (says Taff Price); Gold Ribbed Hare's Ear which is a nice name and is effective almost anywhere; and my favourite, Treacle Parkin, which Taff lists as a Grayling Fly, but which I find deadly for taking trout in fast water.

There is not a fisherman breathing who does not praise his own favourite stream above all others, who does not defend his own methods, and who has not got his own, very special flies. And I am no exception. But I sometimes smile at myself when I walk past one spot on the River Tavy and see small boys fishing there for the trout stocked for them by a benevolent Water Authority. They are spared the agonising choice between Rabley's March Brown and Partridge Glory and Maxwell Red or Blue. What they use, and very successfully, is cheese.

Legend has it that the cheese must be Cheddar — not the plastic kind, but the real thing from Crebers, who have been Pepperers and Cheesemongers in Tavistock since 1881. Discounting the unworthy thought that the legend was begun by the great-grandfather of today's Robert Creber, I think it illustrates the characteristic faith of fishermen in particular *nostra* for particular circumstances. Only such and such a fly will do on such and such a piece of water; only such and such a cheese will bring forth the gourmet trout to its own destruction as the fast-moving Tavy hurries its way through Tavistock Town.

I am never sure. Dr Gowlland* took between 7000 and 9000 flies with him on the last occasion when he went fishing, but did he really need them? And would the small boys who spend their

*See chapter 6 on Paraphernalia Piscatorial.

holidays and weekends fishing below Tavistock's Abbey Bridge get different results if they changed from Yeoman English Cheddar to Continental Brie?

Who knows, and who will ever know the truth? Half the fun of fishing lies in its shibboleths and rituals. Amicable and learned discussion about the relative merits of different baits and lures has gone on since fishing began, and will almost certainly continue to go on until its end, to be taken up thereafter with St Peter. One has to have something to talk about when the season closes and the pubs begin to light their winter fires.

If most of us like to discuss our methods, Fernley Warne, my first true mentor in the ways of Dartmoor fish, did not: not, at least, until he had established that you were a genuine fisherman. Once that was decided to his satisfaction, he was a generous tutor. He taught me everything about his favourite flies, and when and where to use them, and I cherish the knowledge he imparted. Sometimes, though, I suspected he could have caught trout with a bent pin at the end of a cricket stump, since he knew every nook and cranny of the East Dart near Postbridge, and every single remaining fish (after he had taken what he wanted) which lurked in them.

Fernley was a superb fisherman. He was known, universally, as 'Swifty', from his nickname, 'Dean Swift'. This in turn, said his cousin, had come from a racehorse, rather than any connection with the illustrious Irish author. But 'Swifty' certainly displayed some Irish characteristics. He loved good crack over good beer and he loved racehorses, either or both of which *amours*, perhaps, led to him losing his job as a water-bailiff. Above all, he loved fishing.

We had first met in the inn at Postbridge and had found, after some preliminary translation, for his accent was strongly rooted in the Devonshire countryside, that we shared some mutual passions. He, too, loved Dartmoor and the fishing it offered; he, too, loved its solitudes and the constantly changing moods of the local rivers, particularly the East Dart; and he, too, loved the challenge of taking trout which are stream-wise and elusive.

Visiting anglers found Swifty's fund of local lore deeply

fascinating, and his percipience almost uncanny. Once he had accepted you, and you in turn had learned his ways, he was a first-class communicator and teacher, infinitely patient. I shall always remember him with Johnny Rawlings, a Surgeon-Admiral of considerable worldly distinction, though on the river, it has to be said, just another fisherman. He and Swifty spent hours together. 'There, master,' Swifty would say to him. 'Watch the eddy beside that riffle. That's where best 'un 'll be.' And sure enough, 'best 'un' always was.

Swifty knew that fish, like humans, had their own pecking order. The strongest always took the best pool, with the best lie and the most food, and when it was caught, the next strongest fish would take its place. Knowing this, Swifty could find fish when others could not: those who listened to his advice rarely came back with an empty bag.

Swifty is missed. So, too, is my other and very different exemplar, Bunny Spiller, a gentleman of apparently independent, though modest means, whose fishing was both highly unorthodox and very productive.

Bunny was a very tall, thin man, and when he spoke to his friends in Chagford Cattle Market he would bend over like an attenuated question mark in order to hear their less elevated news and views. His everyday dress was that of an Edwardian country gentleman, smart and practical: good, well-polished boots; thick woollen stockings; cord britches; an amply cut, thornproof sports coat with large pockets, worn with a collar and tie, and a matching cap. He rarely ventured out without a crook, and I doubt whether he had ever appeared, unshaven, at breakfast, in the whole of his life. He represented a knowledgeable rural class which has now almost disappeared.

I mostly used to see him on the Cherrybrook, a cheerful stream with its source among the wild hill slopes around White Tor. From there, it bubbles south through Powder Mills, turns east to run alongside Bellever Forest and eventually joins the West Dart below the Ashburton–Tavistock Road to the south-east of Two Bridges. It is an interesting and attractive river to fish, for while it looks somewhat unpromising on first sight, it will provide an occasional trout which is rather larger than one would expect.

Bunny's fishing technique in the broadest sense was not unlike Swifty's, in that he usually fished upstream, using the

Bunny Spiller, gentleman of the Moor

'drowned fly'. I never saw him wading, although the Cherry-brook, with its deep and unexpected rocky pools, is not much of a wading river. Standing several yards back from the bank, and using a small brook rod which looked rather absurd in the hands of someone so tall, he would cast so that only his leader fell onto the water. He would then go down either on one knee or both, first working the tail of the pool and then the underhang on either bank. Sometimes he would not even see the fly, but would strike by instinct at the darting rise of the small trout whose habits he knew so well. As fast as the fish were, he was even faster, sometimes propelling the smaller ones over his shoulder at the speed of light, picking off fish like plastic ducks in a shooting gallery.

When occasionally he hooked something heavier than the average, he would rise to his full height, with arm and rod outstretched above his head, and proceed to play it from this extraordinary position with skill and aplomb. More conventional anglers might observe him with a tolerant, if quizzical smile. But if Bunny did something you could be sure that beneath the apparent madness lay a highly effective method. More than once, in these swift and narrow waters, I have followed his seemingly curious example with much profit.

Bunny was as successful a fisherman as Swifty. The main difference between them was that Bunny tended to return most of his catch while Swifty, perhaps more financially pressed, or simply because he loved the taste, preferred his between two pieces of bread. From both of them, I learned much. And I look back on those summer days spent on the moor with great pleasure. I had not then become a River Warden, but I was trying to paint for a living, and in the search for subjects I spent many, perhaps too many hours, tramping the rivers of the high moors with the zest of a latter-day Izaak Walton. I became absorbed in fishing to the detriment of my pocket and my financial future. I was carefree in every sense but the economic.

Bunny's Cherrybrook — for in a curious way I looked upon it as his river — once yielded me a three-pounder, a fish much larger than most people have ever taken there. I caught it not by rod or line or net, but inadvertently by trap, and not even by fish trap.

It happened in the winter of 1973, when a friend, Paul Channin, was making detailed studies of mink for his Ph.D. thesis at Exeter University. One night he rang to say that he had captured a rare specimen of grey mink on the Teign, near Fingle Bridge, and wondered if I would agree to draw it for him. I was intrigued, for mink are shy and hard to spot: I had not seen many. I told him to bring it over, and was subsequently rewarded by a close-up view of this beautiful, but large and aggressive animal. I looked forward to sketching it. Meanwhile, I had the problem of securely housing it, eventually settling on an old ferret hutch as a suitable cage.

I had forgotten the strength of a mink's powerful jaws. When I checked next morning, the mink had gone. Not bothering to squeeze through the front bars, it had simply gnawed its way out of the wood at the back. Paul, when I told him, was not pleased. Indeed, he was distinctly upset at the idea of a mink caught in one locality being loose in another. He would come over, he said, with his mink traps as soon as he could. I felt very guilty.

Our first problem was to find enough bait for thirty traps. We settled on Kit-E-Kat, a light, domestic cat food of indeterminate vintage not previously employed or advertised as an enticer of wild mink, and began to put the traps along the river. The evening was dry but dark, with threatening clouds: I placed high hopes on two traps which I sited above a deep pool which might, I thought, be attractive to a terrestrial animal with an instinct for water. Lures in place, we retired to our respective beds well content with our work.

During the night, the Dartmoor rains came in sheets. I knew, without leaving my cottage, that the river would have risen by a couple of feet and that the traps, caught in the roaring spate, would most probably be floating down the Dart on their turbulent way to the sea. I rang Paul again, with a heart as heavy as I guessed his to be. Again he was not overjoyed, but he hurried over to help retrieve some of the damage. In the event, we had to wait until the next day for the water level to fall before we could begin our work.

Gloomily, we set out for the swollen river, brightening up only when we saw that some traps, at least, were not lost but had been caught in the debris round Cherrybrook Bridge. Steadily and methodically, though with little expectation that we would find the mink, we worked our way upstream. Suddenly, to Paul's immense relief, we came across our quarry, tetchily secured in a trap set on high ground which the flood had failed to reach. Clever enough to sense the coming of the storm-water, and to keep away from the impending spate, it had not been clever enough to resist the cat food. It gave us a baleful stare, clearly unhappy that it had behaved so foolishly.

Paul carried it off, but there were still more traps to retrieve. I pressed on towards one I had placed under the Clapper Bridge, near Powder Mills. From a distance, I could just see it lying on the bank above the water line. As I trudged over the wet turf, I reflected that I had caught some good trout there in the past, but only by casting upstream and giving the fish a mere split second to rise and take. It was an unsuitable place for normal casting, and most fishermen avoided it as being hard to work.

This time, however, it had yielded its treasure without a fight. Lying in the trap was a superb and quite fortuitous prize, a three-pound brownie, the largest Cherrybrook trout I had ever seen, much less caught. As the waters rose, temporarily covering the trap, it must have swum in to take the bait and, when the water fell, found that it couldn't get out. I could hardly complain if my lucky gift horse were uglier than most of its smaller cousins, with an over-large head and black patches round its gills, since these defects made no intrusion, subsequently, upon my taste buds.

In confessing to the manner in which my happy supper was taken, I hope that the Flyfishers' Lords of Appeal Extraordinary will view my unsporting capture with some sympathy. Firstly, it was an accident. And second, I only bring the tale into the open to confirm that small Dartmoor streams are deceptive. During the years I lived near Mortonhampstead, I came to realise that many are more productive than their appearances may suggest. I ought not to have been surprised at such a monster find, for trout survive in these upland streams in greater numbers than strangers imagine. Finding them, however, is a matter of instinct and experience.

Many trout which go up to the high moors in November remain there for some time, to repair themselves after spawning. Provided the conditions are right, that is provided there is a steady rise in spring temperatures, not too much water, and the fish are beginning to move to the active fly life, then early fishing on streams like the Swincombe and Cowsic can be very gratifying. All you need to enjoy it, apart from a little luck, is easily garnered: a light trout rod, a Duchy Permit from the Forest Inn at Hexworthy and a taste for freedom. There is a special exhilaration in exploring these upland streams, and even in the most unpromising of them it is possible to experience some excellent fishing.

Once, casting gently on the Dart, a few feet above what I could have sworn was a good trout, feeding, as I thought, on a hatch of gnat, I hooked an aberrant salmon. Aberrant because salmon are not supposed to feed in this kind of water, nor to dimple like small trout. I was neither properly equipped, nor licensed by the proper authority, nor ready to take him. I had a two-pound cast and thoughts of larger glory than a small brownie were far from my contented mind. But I am a fisherman not much different from any other. The challenge of a ten-pounder, which was what I judged him to be, was impossible to resist. Despite the odds against me, I determined to land him.

When I struck, he went off like a rocket downstream, towards Dartmouth and the freedom of the English Channel. I sped after him, hanging on to my rod like an old lady trying to restrain a concupiscent dog. My angler's mind worked overtime, and I remembered one pool where, if everything held, I might just have some chance of controlling him. But despite some pretty footwork, with rod held aloft like Bunny Spiller, I failed to stem his outraged progress. He plunged on. Then, about a mile and a half from where I had precipitately abandoned my net and creel, he tired of his sport, leapt into the air in a dazzling arc, and snapped the cast. With one bound, like a thousand Boy's Own heroes before him, he was free.

But I didn't really mind, since his escape was well-merited. And anyway, I should have had to put him back even if I had caught him. The chase was enough in itself, and I trudged back to my abandoned tackle quietly satisfied, although shaking with delayed excitement. Such glorious moments are rare and endlessly pleasant to relive: they more than repay those frustrating days when lines get snagged and all goes wrong.

The Walkham, or at least the trees which fringe its banks downstream of Merrivale Bridge, can snag lines. But it is magnificent fishing, full of 'pots and guts' (a local term for the deep holes and gulleys scoured out of the granite by the force of fast-moving moor water) which provide rich lies, and even richer riffles in which to find a host of good trout.

I fish it by a 'hook and drag' method of my own invention, using a two-fly cast with a big dry dropper which forces the tail-fly to fish more deeply. In this fast water, dry flies serve just as well, without floatant, as wet flies. I fish across and down, letting the strong current swirl them round enticingly, so that the dangle gives the trout a little more time than usual to seize the fly. Unlike their more cossetted chalk-stream cousins, Walkham trout have little time to examine their food before they take it. They have to grab for it quickly, before it is gone.

This method will not be found in the text books, but it is effective. So, too, on this river, is fishing with the often despised

Curlew in flight

worm. Not, of course, just sticking the worm into a pool and waiting for something to happen, like children on the end of a pier, but working the worm with skill and knowledge. To succeed at this, you need to read the river, know the lie of your quarry and be able to cast, very accurately, so as to fall just upstream of him. It is not easy. I do it with a longish rod — a Richard Walker Mark IV Avon — a small fixed-spool reel, a two-pound line and, since I return much of my catch, a number 8 hook too big for the trout to swallow. Using this is the equivalent of using a barbless hook for 'catch and release' fly-fishing, provided you strike correctly.

Sometimes it produces a full bag when flyfishers go home empty-handed: at others, they succeed when the worm fisher-man does not. But it is all part of 'the art of the Angle', and not one which Walton would despise.* Just be sure, before you try it, that you are not infringing any local by-law and, if the stretch is privately owned, that the owner has no objection to the practice.

I was lucky. After my time in Mortonhampstead, I had rented a cottage less than half a mile from the stretch of the Walkham belonging to my then landlord, Colonel Owen Collier, ex-Indian Army Officer and nonagenarian gentleman. He was not himself an angler, but his land covered some two miles of this wonderful river. It was virtually unfished, and he let me fish it. Armed with his courteous letter of authority, I felt I was the most fortunate man in England. Where else could I have found a charming cottage and some of the best fishing in the West Country within my modest means? Where else could I have found such an upright and generous landlord?

If you want to be happy, says the old Chinese proverb, learn to fish. If you want to be even happier, learn to fish for Dartmoor trout. Even the Nirvana induced by a glass of the Colonel's home-brew is hardly matched by a day on the upland streams, 'just fishing'.

---

*See *The Compleat Angler*, Fourth Day, for a definitive discussion on the merits of different worms and how to use them.

6
Paraphernalia Piscatorial

When I was first seized by the love of serious fishing, I would set out on a Saturday morning for the Long Pond, near Tunbridge Wells, with a high heart and enough equipment to tackle anything from a minnow to a small whale. Fellow-passengers in the train from St Paul's Cray, themselves encumbered with the buckets and spades of English families en route to the sea-side, would edge away from me as I sat down, lest they be speared by a knife which sported everything from a disgorger to an implement for removing sharks' fins.

I was festooned in gear, and weighed down by ancillaries. Nothing less than five large loaves, or so I anxiously thought, would see me through a weekend's ground-baiting on the placid waters which awaited me, and my holdall was bursting with weights, floats, ledgers, hooks and swim feeders to suit every condition of pond and stream between the Avon and the Amazon.

I suspect that most of us, once we can afford more than jam-jars and bent pins, begin like that. And some Midlands coarse-fishing match-men, stern-faced fellows who think nothing of spending several weeks under large wet umbrellas beside the torpid Waveney, continue in the same way throughout their lives. Only those of us who fish upland Dartmoor, where the boulders seem to become more rugged, and the marshlands more clogging as the years go on, learn, although reluctantly, to shed all but the most essential appurtenances of the chase.

The obsession with tackle and gadgets never totally leaves us. All fishermen are natural magpies: collectors of unconsidered trifles, and hoarders of broken bits which one day, soon, we are going to clean and mend. We keep and cherish everything we have ever used: old knives, with blades sharpened to slivers of bright steel, battered bait boxes, and accessories long outmoded. We throw away nothing.

Some of us, therefore, become collectors almost by accident. But many others are drawn to amass things for aesthetic reasons. For in parallel with their delight in nature, fishermen also cherish tools and artefacts which are well made. They enjoy the feel of a finely balanced rod, and relish the smooth running of a good reel. They like the craftsmanship of turned brass, and the workman-like neatness of an old-fashioned fly-box. They appreciate things whose beauty is enhanced rather than diminished by the passing of time.

I have written earlier that I felt my first stirrings as would-be collector when I bought my first float. I was fascinated by its visual appeal, by its colour and shape, and I enjoyed simply having it, to admire and hold, much as a Chinese mandarin might handle a piece of rare jade. And I still feel the same

Hardy Curate given to me by my friend Nick

emotions, years later, when I touch what is possibly my favourite fishing item, the Curate, given to me by my good friend, Nick Marchant-Lane, on condition that I never re-sell it at any price. The Curate, to quote the Hardy's catalogue of 1914, was

> an ingenious combination of angler's tools, comprising (1) Tweezers, useful as a disgorger or fly holder; (2) Gut Cutter; (3) Reservoir, to hold oil for dry flies or reels; (4) Stiletto, used to apply oil, or clean the eye of the fly. The handle is milled as a match striker, or small 'priest'.

The price was six shillings, and according to Melner and Kessler,* hundreds were produced for Christmas and as 'thankyou' presents. The workmanship, as one would expect from Hardy's, is exemplary.

Hardy's early catalogues are full of artefacts to delight any fisherman. They show beautiful little oil bottles, just right for the waistcoat pockets of the day; metal fly-driers in the form of a Hunter Watch; the Wardle Magnifier, fixed onto the jacket with a safety pin; tidy fly-boxes and dozens of other delights, such as a water telescope and what was described as a 'very handy little tool', the Magnetic Fly Holder and Scissors (Combined). All of these incunabula were neat, practical and well made: all are eminently collectable by anyone who knows, from his own fishing experience, exactly how they would have been used.

Although my own imagination had initially been caught by a fairly ordinary float, I soon began to concentrate on reels, having been drawn to them by one contrivance in particular; a Dickensian specimen with a loop foot, which fixed onto the rod with a brass wing-nut. It was typical of its period, brilliantly designed and engineered, and solidly executed. The craftsman-ship of this reel, and of some of the Hardy products in which I later specialised, was stunningly good. Handling them still gives me an almost sensual pleasure.

The variety of rods and reels produced in the nineteenth

Great Fishing Tackle Catalogues of the Golden Age, ed. Samuel Melner & Hermann Kessler, with commentary by A.W.Miller, Crown Publishers Inc., New York, 1972.

century, and the numbers of firms producing them, were bewildering. London then was less international than it now is; rents were lower, and small firms producing high-quality goods could afford to operate from the central areas of the West End. There were tackle shops and small manufactures in places like Regent Street, Conduit Street, Jermyn Street, the Strand, Fetter Lane (one, by coincidence, occupied the building in which I first worked in advertising), Haymarket and Piccadilly. On such sites, they were conveniently placed to attract the custom not merely of the gentry, but perhaps even more importantly, of the rising numbers of professional men who were taking up fishing as a serious sport.

Izaak Walton wrote *The Compleat Angler* in the seventeenth century, but the tackle-makers whose names subsequently became known throughout the Empire, if not the world, were largely the product of the bustling nineteenth. Their market was assured, and expanding. The new middle classes had money, and were anxious to do things according to what they perceived as the proper form. The new railways encouraged them to travel, and public opinion supported the pursuit of outdoor activities. If the Fly Fishers' Club was only founded in 1884, talk of it had been in the air for twenty years previously, and angling had been growing in popularity for even longer than that.

Fishing, in short, was a very Victorian pastime, and Victorian entrepreneurs were quick to supply its needs. Firms like Farlow; Little; Baker; Alfred; Blacker, and many more, produced reels which went all over the world. Hardy Brothers of Alnwick, perhaps the most famous of the rod makers, did not start making their own reels until quite late in the century but, when they did, their new patent Perfect reel was widely acclaimed.

Some of the equipment, and the reels in particular, produced by these firms, rank as works of art. For the Victorian tackle-makers had a strong sense of design as well as being both ingenious and down-to-earth in their engineering. They took nothing for granted, and every small part and screw was meticulously fashioned for its particular purpose. We can only marvel that such prosaic things, destined for everyday use (and often rough use, at that) should also be so elegantly wrought.

Many examples of fine Victorian craftsmanship were brought together for the first time in the One Man — One Rod Exhibition at the British Engineerium in Brighton in 1982. This exhibition was a fisherman's paradise of early and late rods, reels and tackle; a visual feast about which collectors like myself still dream. Few of us who saw it, I suspect, will easily forget the solid-silver salmon fly reel made by I.K.Farlow for the Great Exhibition of

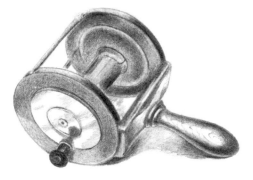

Rare Scottish hand-trolling winch or Pirn

1851. It was, to quote from the catalogue which lies in front of me, a 'type of reel very typical of the period, in as much as it has a turned ivory-handled folding crank wind, with turned screw latch and plate locking register, raised check housing on the back plate and hand shaped foot'. It was also beautifully and delicately engraved, as was another outstanding reel dating from 1830 by a clockmaker, William Dann*. This one was a 'brass trout reel with counterbalanced pierced blued steel crank, a turned ivory handle and spring drag', the spool being the 'earliest known example of a lantern or caged drum'. Rather charmingly, the engraving

---

*At any time, many clock-makers made reels, and some used brass clock-faces in making them.

Cormorant

Robin Armstrong

showed a father and son fishing together.

The technicalities may not excite all fishermen, but few would not admire the look and feel of the actual product. And even the least mechanical of anglers would surely be intrigued by a reel marked as 'Fredk. Skinner's Archimedian Reel', designed for mounting on either side of a rod, and having, among other features, a turned ivory handle and a variable rim spring brake check.

Dozens of such intriguing designs were turned out by the many reel-makers of the time, and to try to collect examples of them all would be impossible. I therefore decided, at a fairly early stage in my collector's progress, to concentrate on the output of Hardy Brothers of Alnwick. This firm, blessed with a goodly number of skilled cabinet-makers among its original employees, had begun making high-quality split-cane rods in 1872. Within ten years, its name was known and respected in angling circles throughout the world. And being lucky enough to own one of their early products, I can understand why.

In their beginnings, Hardy Brothers must have bought their reels from the burgeoning manufacturers in the Midlands. Then, in the early 1890s, Forster Hardy, the engineer of the family, invented the Patent Perfect. It was a huge success. The basic design, adapted and modified over the years, served Hardy's, and their customers, well. It was universally acknowledged as a Rolls Royce among reels, and it continued, in various guises, for seventy-six years, and even then was reintroduced.

The earliest brass Perfect I have seen is owned by my Alaskan friend and fellow-collector, Mike Cuzak. Neither he nor I, however, can put an exact date on it. It has the characteristic big ball-race of the Number One Perfect, but carries additions which do not relate to the pictures in the early catalogues. And since there is no works book against which to check how many of each design were produced, or when, there is no way — yet — of solving the problem.

It is the 'yet' which supplies the intrigue and adds to the excitement of collecting. Nobody knows if the first Perfect still exists: nobody knows the date of the one owned by Cuzak. But

Otter with 'my' sea trout

someday, somewhere, somebody might just make the discovery which will provide enlightenment. And every collector hopes and dreams that it will be he. This is the charm of the business: the most important find can just as easily be made by an impecunious enthusiast as by a millionaire.

Precisely dateable or not, the early Perfects are still much sought after. Mike Cuzak's specimen is a reel with the usual revolving plate, a detached outside face resting on ball-bearings (which give it a smoother action than many contemporary reels) and a tension screw to increase or decrease the drag when you hooked, or were landing a fish. This feature gives it a claim to being the finest reel ever made.

I would not judge the claim. Indeed, I am not sure that anyone could, since different reels serve different purposes. And anyway, there would be nothing left to argue (amiably) about if all collectors were to make the same choice of number one. Like enthusiasts selecting the finest vintage car, or small boys picking the greatest-ever world cricket eleven, fishermen enjoy making up their own pecking-orders of virtue. Collecting would lose its charm if everyone were to collect the same things.

Towards the end of the nineteenth century, simply deciding which reel to choose for everyday use could not have been easy. Changes and improvements to existing reels were being made continuously: new designs were pouring out from small shops all over the country. In London, Newark, Birmingham and Scotland, groups of makers vied for attention. Some designs and their progenitors sank without a trace, but the fame of others lives on. Mr Malloch of Perth, for example, a famous dealer and the author of an excellent book of early photographs to which I still refer when drawing fish, invented a patent side-caster in 1884 which was still being made in the 1930s.

Few other designs, apart from Hardy's Perfect, achieved such longevity. Yet most early reels, the forerunners of today's fixed spool reels, were made of brass and to a high standard of finish. Even those which failed to achieve fame were good to look at and, despite their weight, easy to use. With them, many a stolid Scots salmon-fisherman, well wrapped against the nineteenth-century elements, could flip his reel drum and flick out a large Devon minnow with every prospect of taking a fish worth more than he had paid in river fees. The unpolluted waters of those days must have been alive with the cries of canny Celts pulling out eighteen-pounders.

Much though I have dabbled in the realms of other makers, I confess that I remain biased towards the Family Hardy (now part of a bigger group). They made some marvellous rods, and even better reels. The Patent Silex, which Canadians and North Americans still use for salmon in big and heavy waters, was a miracle of engineering. The men who fashioned them, by hand, with no two exactly the same, could be compared in skills with precision clockmakers. Their reels, made of Duralamin in the later runs, still look like new pins some fifty or sixty years on.

Everything that Hardy's sold was of fine quality — or perhaps I should say that everything bearing their name which I have known personally seemed truly to reflect the practical fishing experience of their directors. Apart from rods, reels and tackle, and the small artefacts mentioned in earlier pages, they supplied almost every fishing need: knee pads, mosquito nets, smokers' pipes, boots, waders, fly-cabinets, bait-kettles, creels, bags, gaffs, nets, lures, fly-makers' tools, knives of every sort and much else. To browse through the pleasure-garden of their catalogue in the close season almost makes up for the lack of fishing.

And thus, too, with collecting. When the nights are long, and the curtains muffle the sound of winter frets, there is consolation in reviewing what one already has, and dreaming about what, if fortune smiles, one might someday acquire. The price of old gear in the auction houses may be rising to impossible heights for most of us, but there is always the possibility of a lucky find.

Once, coming back from Scotland, we stopped over in the Lake District. Idly, waiting for my wife Anne, I browsed through a junk shop. In a corner, neglected, there was a wooden creel of planed oak ply, with a leather strap: it was green outside and white within, with just the right patina to arouse the collector's instincts.

I bought it, without haggling, for the asking price of £38, and rang my friend and mentor in these matters, Nick Marchant-Lane. He confirmed the wisdom of my purchase, even though paying out that amount, in those days, had left us with hardly enough money to get home. Later, the creel was exhibited at Sothebys, where it was valued at £500.

Late 19th c. French reed creel with leather binding

I revelled for an instant, like Peter Pan, in 'the cleverness of me', but of course I knew that I had simply been lucky, a chance recipient of a favour bestowed by the gods on all collectors at least once in their lives. I had never collected for money, but for love: to make an unexpected profit was a bonus.

Collecting reels gives me great pleasure. But the pleasure is secondary to that which comes from my fishing. And when I had to sell my collection, to take advantage of an opportunity to buy our rented cottage, I did so without qualms. In the two years or so I spent renovating our new freehold, I reflected how easy, and damaging, it would be to become obsessive about what are, after all, only inanimate objects.

At one auction I attended, a fellow-collector had instructed a dealer to bid for a particular reel on his behalf. 'I want it at any price,' he had instructed, and so briefed, the dealer had taken up an unobtrusive place on the floor. The reel was worth about £250, and I dropped out of the bidding at £200, sensing that the dealer was determined to buy. At £250 the rest of the floor dropped out. The dealer was left bidding against a telephone client. The bids grew steadily, the dealer clearly becoming more uncomfortable, but no less determined, as the price rose to £600. The floor, by now, was waiting keenly for the unknown caller to raise his bid. He did. The dealer looked distinctly anxious. He had been instructed to pay 'any price', but commonsense told him that even 'any price' had its limits, and thrice the accepted value was approaching those limits. He dropped out at £800, and the reel went to the telephone bidder.

Later, we found out what had happened. The man who had commissioned the dealer to buy for him had become so intense about his projected acquisition, and so distrustful of his agent, that he had telephoned the saleroom to check that the man was present. The auctioneer's assistant had failed to spot him. So the collector had done his own bidding against the dealer acting on his behalf, and in the process, lost himself some £500. Passionate, distrustful, obsessive, paranoid even; whatever adjective one chooses to use about him, the collector had clearly gone over the top. He had allowed a harmless and interesting pursuit to seize hold of him to the point of idiocy, and I drew my own conclusions from his example.

Auctions can be fun. Waiting for a particular lot, watching who else in the room is likely to be interested in it, and trying to guess how much one might have to bid to get it, races the adrenalin almost as much as playing a big fish. It is agreeable, too, to talk to other collectors and to build on relationships with other enthusiasts in their specialist fields. But I have no delusions of collecting grandeur: I should never become manic about those items which get away, even if I were once found in unseemly embrace with one which did not.

When fishermen are not near rivers, there is a good chance that they will be near a bar, telling stories to other fishermen. At the annual sale of fishing tackle at Stockbridge, which attracts knowledgeable collectors and anglers from all over the country, the bar of the Grosvenor Hotel in the High Street resounds with claims and counter-claims which lose nought in the re-telling.

One year, I took with me a Silex reel acquired from one Stacey Weeks, a cobbler from Oxfordshire who affected a curly-brimmed, brown bowler hat to reinforce his somewhat Edwardian mien. He was well known in fishing circles: an honest man with whom I had done several mutually satisfactory deals over many years. But I was especially grateful to him for the Silex. It was the multiplying version, designed, in the words of Hardy's catalogue of 1931, 'under certain circumstances to recover baits more quickly than can comfortably be done with a single action reel', for example, when fishing some 'dead water' and you want to make the spinner more attractive by moving it quickly. It was the pride of my modest collection, and my personal joy.

There are plenty of Silex reels to be found, but this one was unusual. It had a little pipe down one side which said, 'Oil Me', and it was in excellent condition. As I showed it off, over several evening pints, it drew much seasoned admiration. I basked in the interest it aroused, and unworthily took secret pleasure in the envy expressed in the faces of my peers.

Whether it was the absence of Anne, or the considerable presence of the Hampshire Ale, or simply the fear that I might lose it to an unknown and jealous hand, I cannot soberly say. I only know that I took the reel to bed with me, and played with it, besottedly. Only fellow-fishermen, perhaps, might understand that while turning a reel handle is no substitute for sex, it can be very relaxing.

There was a knock on the door from the adjoining room. Jamie Maxtone-Graham, a well known tackle dealer, had heard the curious sound of the reel and had come in to find out what was going on. I explained, feeling very foolish. 'Don't worry!' he said, 'You're not the first. I once went into Hoagy Carmichael's Jr's room and found him doing exactly the same.'*

All collectors share common lunacies: all are capable of becoming wildly excited over what, to an outsider, may look like nothing but a chunk of old brass. My friend Mike Cuzak would

---

*Carmichael is a renowned collector of reels from all over the world.

telephone regularly from Alaska, almost always choosing the wrong time, so that I was woken in mid-sleep. Had I heard about his latest acquisition, he would ask, and then spend a very expensive hour describing it. His collection at King Salmon Lodge, above one of the bays of the same name, is said to be one of the finest in the world, but, sadly, I have never seen it. He offered to fly me there once but, even from one of his great wealth, the gesture seemed too extravagant. With dust and ashes in my mouth, I politely declined his generous offer.

Cuzak, like me, collects reels. Others, particularly the Americans, collect lures, while the Europeans take a greater interest in tackle. The list of things sold by Jamie Maxtone-Graham, from his home in Scotland, encompasses everything from old fishing diaries to bait boxes, all, no doubt, with their specialist collectors. When one member of the Fly Fishers' Club, Dr Peter Gowlland, died, he was found to have left '367 rods, (and) a billiard room festooned with floats strung across the table, while his salmon flies ran into thousands and his trout flies into hundreds of thousands, and there was other gear to match'.*

Madmen all, perhaps, except that fishermen tend to be less disruptive of the Queen's Peace, and more contented, and longer-lived than most ordinary mortals. If they like to collect some of the finer examples of the tackle used in pursuing their elusive quarry, who shall gainsay them?

Three hundred and sixty seven rods is, I admit, a trifle excessive: my own ambitions have always been more modest. In my previous collection I had one rod by Leonard's of Maine,** considered by some to be the best of the American bamboo rod-makers, but to collect such rods in any number would be difficult and expensive. I contented myself with that, and enjoyed having

*See *The Book of the Flyfishers' Club 1884–1934* (published privately by the Club?), p.19.

**For the technical: the cane tapered into the rod from the cigar-shaped handle. It had ruby whipping and nickel silver fittings. I regret that only some of the early Hardys could compare favourably with it.

it, but reels remained my first love and I was not overly upset when I had to sell it.

On reels, with deference to a host of more expert collectors, I am moderately knowledgeable: with rods, I should have to begin the learning process all over again. I prefer to swop and deal, in a small way, with those things which I know and understand. It is highly satisfying to go to a sale and to have some idea of the likely prices, even if I shall probably never reach the canny precisions of Nick Marchant-Lane. I recall being with him at one sale where he was hoping to get a stuffed trout. The bids went on up to £150. I thought it strange that he wouldn't buy at one bid higher, since I knew he badly wanted it. He looked at me disbelievingly; 'That,' he said, in injured tones, 'is how much it's worth!'

And that, in a phrase, summed up the difference between the professional dealer and the amateur collector. I had no wish to cross the divide. I have spent many happy hours browsing through flea markets and standing at auctions, and I hope to spend many more, but I shall be doing so for love, not in the hope of monetary gain. I travel hopefully towards the find of a lifetime, but I shall not be disappointed when I fail to arrive.

Provided one approaches collecting in that spirit, it can be an absorbing and more than enjoyable hobby. But it must never be allowed to progress from hobby to obsession. Nor will it ever replace in thrills and satisfaction the main business of being on the river at the evening rise. 'There is nothing, absolutely nothing,' said Ratty, 'half as much worth doing as simply messing about in boats.' But he was wrong. He can never have stood, with the right rod, and the right line, at the right time, in the right place, on the right river. Using, of course, the right reel.

7

Nature's Fishermen

The sky changes from grey to blue, and the earth from green to sun-dried brown, but living nature, in all its sharpened tooth and claw, is always deepest red. In every pool and cranny of every placid stream, copse and field of rural England, slaughter never ceases. The idea of a peaceful countryside, 'where every prospect pleases and only man is vile', is a myth. Practically every other living thing is also vile, and even the cheerful robin, our national bird, is not warmly regarded by earthworms.

Fish eat other forms of life and other fish, and in turn are themselves eaten — as much by natural predators as by anglers. The otter feels no pangs of vegetarian misgiving when it dines off a small trout, and it is likely to be some time before anyone persuades bass to give up sprats. All in all, the natural world is brutish.

Very few humans are equipped to dive gracefully into fretful waters and emerge clutching a fish, but our rivers and shores are alive with creatures which can do precisely that. And over many years, I have watched them doing so with as much pleasure as I have derived from fishing on my own account.

Some creatures, like the otter, I have seen in action only rarely, and by happy chance: others, like gulls, I see almost every day. But however frequent or sporadic my sightings, I never tire of them. A motionless heron, patiently waiting for an early morning trout, is an enchanting sight; so, too, in a totally different way, are gannets dive-bombing the seas off Kintyre in search of herring.

The very essence of angling is the opportunity it affords to look upon nature with a quiet eye. Those few fishermen who are blind to the wildlife around them are losing much of fishing's pleasure. Even those city-dwellers who stoically probe the murky Thames from the old wharves near Greenwich, never expecting to catch anything much but an occasional eel, gain solace from the sight of the river birds, wheeling down on to some discarded urban tid-bit.

To fish only for the sake of catching fish would be a poor sport: in the South-West, the variety of wildlife adds a bonus to every fishing day. People are less obtrusive than in many places, and the countryside is less domesticated: there are still some rivers free from poisons, and some paths which remain untramped by tourist boots. For lovers of the natural world, much remains to be enjoyed.

For an angler, there is always interest in watching other creatures do instinctively what he only succeeds in doing by art and craft. Nature's fishermen abound in the South-West, some-times to an excessive degree, and a river warden sees them every day. On the estuaries, sea-birds fish continuously, diving down in great, flamboyant swoops for all to watch. On the rivers, animals and birds are more circumspect and harder to spot. But they are ever-present and, sooner or later, the patient observer will be rewarded by a sight of them on their daily shopping rounds.

Perhaps the rarest, and the hardest to spot, is the otter, a shy creature which is less able to live easily alongside man than the commoner feral mink. Like the red squirrel, overwhelmed by its grey and plebeian cousins, the otter has been driven away to the extremes of our rural landscape. Nowadays, you mostly see it on the Hebridean Islands and the west coast of Scotland. In England, where it was once extensively hunted,* it is now rare.

That it was hunted is, I suppose, understandable, for it has a large appetite for fish and is powerfully adapted to taking salmon and trout from the rich rivers of the South-West. Its under-fur is very thick, and its guard hairs (the top hairs in a mammal) are oily, so that air is trapped between the layers and the animal, well insulated, can swim sleekly in the coldest of water. Aquadynami- cally, its progress is aided by webbed toes and elongated rear feet which act as propellers. Its tail, thick at the base and long and tapering, is a further help to fast racing turns, and its nostril, which opens and closes by muscular movement, so that it can keep out water, allows it to achieve considerable underwater staying power.

But I am no expert. I see the countryside as an amateur field naturalist; an interested observer rather than an academic.** Most of my knowledge of otters comes from seeing the small population on the Cherrybrook. There, if you dare to brave the Dartmoor night, and you are patient, you might hear their distinctive whistling, like the mewing of cats. You can then confirm their location in daylight by looking for their droppings (spraints), often placed on rocks in mid-river and, if you are lucky, you might see them at play, sliding down into the water from mud-chutes they construct themselves.

One night, while waiting to fish on Queenie Pool, a popular sea-trout holding pool on the Dart River, where fishermen allow themselves only twenty minutes' fishing before giving way to the next in the queue, I heard the distinctive fluting whistle of an otter. It was a young one, I thought, but I dared not switch on my torch to check, lest I 'spook' my fellow-angler's fish. So I waited.

*For various reasons, I support the ban on otter hunting. But I confess that I find otter hounds among the most attractive of English field dogs.

**For a learned over-view of otters, see the works of H.G.Hurrel and Paul Channin. *British Mammals* by Harrison Matthews is also worth reading — if you can find a copy.

The man in front of me went off (having taken four good fish) and I took over. Within minutes, I was into a small sea-trout which, following the usual pattern, immediately took off up-stream. I followed to where it had stopped between two rocks. From the curve in my rod, I knew it was not a very large fish. Suddenly, however, it became very heavy, as though I were roach-fishing and my roach had been grabbed by a big pike. Something had clearly snagged my fish. There was a flurry in the water: the line went slack and I could hear much splashing. When I switched on my torch, I saw a young otter holding a sea-trout with a line dangling from its mouth.

The otter glared balefully into the beam of the torch, resentful of the strange light which had come between him and his supper, then slipped off into the Devonshire night. But he did let go of the fish, which I managed to retrieve in one piece.

An unremarkable story? Perhaps. But otters, though beautiful, and brave and tenacious enough to drag hounds into water in order to drown them, are not normally so incautious,* and I wondered whether this had ever happened before? I would have expected this one to swim away at the very first evidence — the sound of my stumbling steps as I followed my trout upriver — of a human presence. Outside of nature reserves and zoos, otters are uncommonly difficult to meet: I felt privileged to have seen this one at work, in the wild, at such close quarters.

I was also privileged to watch another natural fisherman, the kingfisher, at very close quarters, as he, too, went about his methodical kill. Again it was by chance: had I set out to watch

---

*In an introduction to Henry Williamson's *Tarka the Otter*, 1978 edition, Richard Williamson quotes the records of the Cheriton Otter Hunt.

In 1923, when there were many more otters in the West Country than there are now, the hunt met on 61 occasions and only found otter 33 times. Yet the distance walked must have been over 1000 miles.

Henry Williamson himself records having had the 'great good fortune to watch several otters hunting salmon in the pool' (below the bridge at Taddiport). He would hardly have noted this if the sight had been common-place. One would also have expected the hunt, deliberately searching in known otter haunts and helped by hounds, to have made more sightings than one in every thirty miles walked.

him, I doubt if I should have seen him perform his dramatic ritual in such detail. For usually this beautiful bird is shy and fast-moving: quite often, all you see of him is an iridescent streak as he moves away at the sound of your coming.

I know of several pairs of these birds on the Walkham and the Tavy, where they nest in holes (which stink of rotten fish) in the riverbank, and I have seen them fish on many occasions.

Medway kingfisher

Sometimes they bellyflop from a hover, but mostly they wait motionless on a rock or bough until they spot their prey and then dive like gannets below the water to pick up some small trout or minnow. Predators rarely bother them since they eat only aquatic things and their flesh is no doubt too foul-tasting to be attractive.

The one which I saw closest came to me uninvited. I was fishing pike, on the Medway at Yalding, not thinking about anything very much except my new fishing outfit; a full-length tank suit, the *de rigueur* uniform of the trendiest 1960s' specimen hunters. I felt myself, immodestly, the cynosure of the river: the very model of good fishing form.

I was not. My visitor was much more brilliantly tailored than I in a blue-green tail-coat with orange shirt front, nicely set off by little white patches at the throat and sides of the neck. He was Turnbull and Asser to my Marks and Spencer, and he knew it. With amazing boldness, he plonked down on the end of my rod, defying me to shift him, and set about his mission. His purpose was serious: he wasted no time in preening. For some minutes, he studied the water intently: then he dived in and came up holding a small bleak in his bill, head-first, in case he swallowed it too soon.* Back on the end of my rod, he tossed the fish in the air, like an Olney housewife with a pancake, and deftly caught it by the tail on its way down. He then hammered it against the rod to stun it, turned it round, and swallowed it. It was a marvellous performance, instinctive and economical, but not without a dash of bravura. Under other circumstances, I would have clapped.

Because they rely almost exclusively on water life for their food, kingfishers suffer very badly in severe winters. When the east wind bites, and the upper pools freeze over, many die. Herons also suffer, because their normal prey — eels, fish and small mammals — are either beneath the ice or dormant. In the winter months, dead herons, stiff beside some frozen pool, are a sadly common sight.

In summer, they flourish, adding enchantment to every rural scene they choose to grace, and touring city-dwellers who see them fishing account themselves lucky. Mostly, they stand patiently on one leg, waiting to stab approaching fish with their strong, razor-like bills, but sometimes they splash through the shallows to pick off whatever they can find. They may even leave the relative safety of the river to seek small mammals in cornfields or hayricks if necessary, but eels are their preferred and staple diet.

I enjoy the sight of herons, as I enjoy the sight of most birds. Trout farm owners, and people with valuable fish in ornamental ponds, are understandably less enthusiastic about them. But the

---

*If the fish were swallowed tail-first, the fins and scales would open as they went down and choke the bird. A bleak (or blay) is a small river-fish or allied sea-fish.

grand houses and the monasteries, cultivating their carp for winter feasts, managed to live with them,* and I think we can afford to do the same As far as anyone knows, the heron population has remained relatively stable over the past sixty years (declining, of course, after severe winters), so that their demands on human resources cannot have been excessive. Certainly if we were to lose too many to enthusiastic guns, our rural aesthetics would be diminished, for they are an immensely attractive sight on any stretch of water.

Herons live in noisy, bawling high-rise communities in nests built of heavy sticks, at the tops of tall trees. Elsewhere, they seek silence and solitude. In my early days as a River Warden, I was told they guarded their patch so effectively that to see one rising was a sign that no one was on the river. But I have proved this wrong, by once stalking one until I could almost touch it, so intent was it on its fishing.

Cormorants in large numbers I might find less easy to champion, for they can devastate any fishery they pick upon for easy snacks. It has been said that a cormorant can eat an eel, 2½-feet long, or consume in a day more than its own weight in fish, choking down, crudely, more than good manners would ever deem acceptable.

Cormorants mostly nest on rocks and ledges on the coast and feed inshore, on flatfish and the like. In theory, therefore, they constitute no threat to inland fisheries. But they often do leave their estuaries, particularly if there is a heavy smolt migration, to fly upriver, inelegantly food-shopping from pool to pool, like greedy day-trippers. Out of the water, they are ungainly birds, bathetic and uncouth, reminding me of talentless music-hall comedians who never know when to leave the stage. I watched one, once, foolishly knock itself out on a disused iron footbridge over the Tavy. As I approached, it rose awkwardly and tried to hop over the bridge to the next pool. It failed, and struck an old iron support chain with a fearsome clang. Had I been able to

---

*Because they could defend themselves aggressively, it was once considered good sport to hunt them with falcons. But not, I think, by any of my forbears.

reach it before it flew off, I would have killed it, since it was doing powerful damage to the migrating spring smolts.

The Water Authority takes its conservation role very seriously. Thus, early in my River Warden's career, I had no qualms about being ordered to take part in a cormorant shoot. No mass slaughter was envisaged. The target was a single bird; a lone raider which was attacking our fish cages on Tamar lake, near Bude, and killing up to twenty trout a day through the net meshes.

The Warden was not a shooting man, so a small party of us had been assembled to rid the water of this renegade bird, all efforts to scare him off having failed. We were a disparate group, chosen not wisely but at random. I had been recruited because of some previous (and minimal) keeping experience, and Harry de Quick was there because of his country knowledge. The only marksman among us with Eddie Aze, nicknamed, for physical reasons, the Launceston Heron, and well known for his love of 'vermin bashing'.

On Eddie's suggestion, we had agreed to be in place before dawn. Shortly after that, he thought, would be the best time for a successful shoot. It would be a rare day away from our normal routine, to be armed, and licensed to kill. But to kill what? Only the Heron had anything like a proper gun. Mine was a single-barrelled Greener which looked as though it had been last used in the Zulu wars. Harry's was even older. I was fearful that it might, if fired, blow up in his face.

We took up our positions like members of Dad's Army. Eddie was to be our Captain Mainwaring, the man to fire the first shot. Harry and I were the support troops, the long-stops should Eddie miss. I was on the right flank, hidden beneath some old fish netting; Harry was the front man, on the parapet of the dam, but out of sight; Eddie was in a hide to the left, closest to the cage.

The cormorant came in at first light, fast and low. It landed in a flurry on top of the cage, croaked mightily and examined the contents. Wasting no time, it then plunged into the water and came up a few minutes later with a big, two-pound rainbow trout in its bill. Now, I thought, was the time to get it, but Eddie, Great White Hunter and Crack-Shot, thought otherwise. He obviously

Rainbow coming to the net

Robin Armstrong

Robin Armstrong

reasoned that the bird would fly more slowly once it had swallowed its weighty prey, and make an easier target in the air than on the water.

We stayed put. The bird began to choke down the fish, with difficulty, making a lot of odd noises as it did so. There were noises, too, from the direction of Harry's parapet hide-away; snoring noises. He had clearly fallen fast asleep.

Young cormorant

By this time, the bird had managed to swallow its monster breakfast. It bobbed in the water, too full to float easily. All I could see of it was its head, barely above the surface and presenting no target to the waiting gun. Eddie's patience ran out. To get a good shot he would have to persuade the bird, weighed down by trout, out of the water. To move it, he began to jump up and down and clap his hands like a fire-walker who had suddenly begun to feel the flames. The bird took off, rather lumberingly, towards the parapet, three feet above the smooth water. I began whistling the Dambusters March, but only for my own amusement, since Harry, sonorously, was still asleep, and Eddie was too busy aiming to notice much else.

Eddie's shooting reputation proved to be not unfounded. He hit the cormorant, in the bottom, with both barrels. Dead in the air, its own momentum increased by the power of bird-shot, it skimmed along the top of the water, bouncing three times in succession like a Barnes Wallis bomb. On its fourth bounce, it landed with a thud on Harry's hide-out.

More precisely, it landed on the sleeping Harry. It was the first time in his life, he said later, and I believed him, that he had been attacked, at dawn, while still asleep, by a dead bird, very wet and smelling of fish. A lesser man might have expired on the spot.

The next thing I saw was a flying cormorant being ejected, very forcibly, from the hide-out, and an archaic shotgun flailing about over Harry's distraught head. He was defending himself vigorously against his unwelcome assailant, not knowing what it was. We could hardly blame him for imagining that he was under threat from something more sinister than a dead bird.

I doubt if I shall easily forget that early morning on the lake, with the sight and sound of Eddie laughing uncontrollably at a desperate Harry; a Harry who was not quite sure what was happening, but was nonetheless prepared to take on all-comers, quick or dead.

We returned to base with the lifeless cormorant strapped over the body of the car, like big-game hunters with a tiger. The Warden was given an official gun and told to shoot his own predators in future. And we, deciding that we made better river-keepers than hit-men, happily returned to the serenities (and the occasional excitements of poacher-chasing) of our daily rounds.

I was not especially proud of my part in the shooting, but nor was I ashamed of it. Conservationists who would preserve every single bird, regardless of what it was doing to other birds, or fish, or crops, are sentimental and unrealistic. We killed one cormorant in order to save a very large number of valuable trout, even if the trout in turn had another fate awaiting them. What we shot was a full member of a tribe of expert fishermen, who can swim faster than most fish, and devastate a fishery almost overnight.

If they stuck to their natural ways perhaps they could be left alone. But once addicted to some handy fish-breeding ground, they become a menace, and must be controlled. In the expensive salmon fisheries of Scotland, cormorants are treated like mink, and slaughtered in profusion. If they were not, then their gluttonous raiding would wreck an important industry.

Perhaps we should follow the example of the Chinese, who train cormorants to fish on human behalf. The birds are banded at the neck, below the crop, so that they can fish but not feed. When they have caught something, they are pulled back to the boat by strings attached to their legs and made to disgorge it. An economical way to fish, I think, saving all the trouble of finding bait, and fiddling with hooks, and waiting for a bite. If it were introduced here, it would not be long before the competition secretaries and the club chairman had the reservoirs full of anglers matching their favourite birds in contests for the biggest take.

Ospreys, which are also efficient fishermen of trout (and pike), once had much the same reputation as cormorants and, because of that, were harried until they had virtually disappeared from Britain by the turn of the century. Reintroduced on to Loch Garten in the 1950s, and carefully protected, they have re-established themselves in a few places, although their future is always under threat from greedy egg collectors, anxious to achieve a rare prize. When fishing, they glide along about thirty feet above the surface of the water then dive down with a great, spectacular splash, not always successfully. I sighted one at work on the Plym Estuary, but I was lucky: normally, the only realistic chance of seeing them would be on Speyside.

Without travelling to Scotland, however, one could follow the example of the poet F.W.Harvey and, 'from the troubles of this world', turn to ducks. They offer much solace, and I turn to them often as marvellous subjects for painting. Many of them, of course, are not strictly fishing birds. Those which are, like goosanders and the beautiful red-breasted merganser, with the characteristic saw-bill (from which fish, once caught, find it hard to wriggle free), are often vilified unfairly. For while they do eat fish, they take relatively few of the anglers' precious trout and salmon.

Obsessive anglers will find enemies of their sport everywhere. I am not one of them. Unless the damage done to stocks by the natural fishermen is excessive, I find the pleasure they give me more than outweighs the loss of the fish which they steal. The bittern, for example, is not going to rob me of much of my potential catch, but the sight of it trying to emulate the reeds among which it likes to lurk is immensely pleasing. When I saw a bittern trying to do this in a patch too thin to provide cover, leaving it bewildered and confused, I felt sorry for it. Who would begrudge it a fish or two?

Divers, too, cause me few fishing worries. They are relatively rare, and in any case they prefer, whenever they can, to eat from salt-water estuaries rather than rivers. They, and birds like the dabchick, are never going to make any serious impression on fish stocks. The dabchick* is too small for anything much bigger than sticklebacks and shrimps, and so ungainly in flight that one feels concerned for him, although the concern disappears once he gets into the water.

The other grebes are more rare. The Great Crested, much hunted in Victorian times to provide feathers for ladies' hats, almost died out in Britain, but has now returned. I saw one, incongruously, on a reservoir beside London Airport, perhaps on its way back to one of the newly landscaped gravel pits in southern Berkshire.

Not all is being lost in the environmental war. The landscaped gravel pits are but one example of the trend towards repairing some of the landscape damage of earlier industrial workings. Birds once feared to be dying out are re-emerging: rivers once grossly polluted are beginning, again, to sustain fish. If not all, at least some of the ravages of past indifference are being put right, and places where no birds sing, and no fish swim, are becoming marginally fewer.

The fishermen among sea-birds have been less harassed than their inland cousins. Gannets, two-thirds of the world's population of which are thought to be hatched in the thirteen gannetries

---

*In Coward's *Birds of the British Isles*, pub. in revised edition, 1975, by F.Warne, they are said to collide with lighthouses during night-time wanderings. Is there, I wonder, any evidence that birds have access to natural alcohol?

of the British Isles, are still with us in their thousands. So are guillemots, and kittiwakes, the prettiest and most delicate of the gulls and perhaps the most efficient of our sea-fishermen. Despite the susceptibility to bad weather of their nests, precariously perched on the very edge of cliffs, their perky tribe seems constantly to increase.

Young red squirrel

All sea-birds are fascinating to watch as they wheel and glide and dive above the ever-surging water. Even those gulls which scavenge rather than fish, and bullies like the piratical skua which frightens others into disgorging their catch, make attractive pictures. I can spend hours viewing their graceful — and sometimes disgraceful — disport. I see them all as fellow-fishermen; an integral part of my angling world. Simply to fish, however successfully, in a sanitised concrete bowl, generates neither excitement nor content.

For me, fishing cannot be separated from the circumstances in which I fish. Freedom of stream and shore; the surrounding wildlife; the birds, the scenery and the weather; all are parts of my angling whole. If I write about natural fishermen it is because they give me much pleasure, and because they help me to feel at one with a greater and unfathomable world outside myself.

But save the mark! Could I honestly swear to behave well, should a cormorant steal the last trout from my favourite pool?

8

Kennet Country

The River Kennet starts in Wiltshire, somewhere to the west of Marlborough, and ends in Berkshire, where it joins the Thames just east of Reading. It is a tiddler among rivers, no more than fifty miles long and nowhere very wide, and barely deep enough for a man to dive into. Compared with the great rivers of the world, with the Ganges or the Amazon, it is a river of no account; a peaceful, gentle waterway which serves little purpose other than to drain the quiet vale through which it calmly flows.

But many an Englishman, too long abroad, will remember the Kennet when he has forgotten much grander sights. The splendour of a tropical sunset, or the grandeur of an Eastern dawn, will not move him as much as the memory of a June morning on the water's edge near Kintbury, waiting for the first rise. For Kennet country is quintessential England, with stolid, dappled cows, heavy with milk, gracing green watermeadows, strong oaks standing in rolling parkland, and sheep safely grazing. It is trailing willows and the scent of honeysuckle, duckponds and church clocks telling slow hours. Kennet country is what all England might have been.

The River Kennet itself is to trout men what Lord's is to cricketers. To fish there is the dream of anyone who has ever wielded a serious fly-rod. Since my earliest fishing days, earnestly perusing Mr Crabtree, I had read of it with much longing but little hope that I would ever fish it. Now, to be invited by my friend, David Channing-Williams, to share his rod while he prepared for the daunting business of his wedding, was bliss indeed.

'What better way to spend my last two days as a bachelor than on the river,' he had said on the telephone. I could think of none. And though I wished him well, and was very happy to act as one of his supporters, I cannot pretend that the wedding took precedence in my thoughts over the feast of fly-fishing which lay ahead for me.

I drove slowly up from Devon on a sparkling day, enjoying the countryside. Anne was to join me later. It was early June and, as was fitting, very warm: when you fish a chalk stream, especially the Kennet, the sun should shine and the summer insects should buzz deafeningly, and the river should be loud with rising trout. I knew when I stopped at Kintbury and saw clouds of wonderful mayfly in greater numbers than I had ever seen them anywhere before, that all I had ever anticipated would turn out to be true.

David, who had wedding rehearsals to attend, would not be with me all the time, but he had arranged that I should try all the various types of fishing offered by both the river itself and its attendant carriers. I would have a busy time. Meanwhile I had to drag myself away from the fantastic sight of a river almost completely covered in myriads of mayfly, like raindrops, and full of trout totally preoccupied with such rich feeding. There was no dissembling: they crashed about everywhere on the surface with very untroutly disregard for their safety. The temptation to get my rod from the car and begin fishing there and then was almost overwhelming, even though I had neither licence nor permit. I had never seen such a sight, and I drove on to David's house quivering with excitement. I was all for going back at once: dinner, I thought, could wait.

David was welcoming, but less ebullient. 'Calm down,' he said. 'Have a drink, and then we might go down for a walk. But there's no point in trying to catch anything. The fish are so busy with all the naturals that they'll never look at an artificial.' He was right of course, and I took his point, albeit reluctantly, for a great part of me, despite all logic, still wanted to be on the river with a rod in my hand.

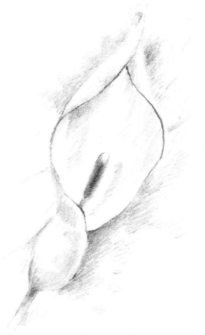

Cuckoo Pint, a familiar waterside plant

David went on, 'You have to choose the right time. Early to mid-morning is probably the best, when there aren't many naturals about. That is, if you really want to "pull up the big ones".' I did. I very much did. So much so, in fact, that I could hardly sleep, and I got up long before anyone else had begun to stir.

To 'pull up the big ones' was a local expression. It referred to the fact that the larger, more 'natural' trout were normally hard to catch, since they tended to stay close to the bottom feeding on large nymphs and other insects. But even the wiliest were tempted to the surface by the astonishly rich and prolific mayfly hatch, allowing the angler almost his only realistic chance of getting a big Kennet trout during the whole season.

The mayfly season itself lasts about two weeks, though at different times in different parts of the river system during early summer. Where I was, it had arrived, spectacularly, in the first week of June. Even as I watched them, the numbers of mayfly seemed to increase: so did their frenetic activity. But this is not perhaps surprising, for their Latin name, *ephemerida*, tells all. A mayfly has at worst a few hours and at best a few days of adult life in which to enjoy itself, after up to three years spent developing under freshwater stones. And even those brief moments of glorious life might be cut short, on the Kennet, by an avaricious trout.

Next morning's early rising did me little good. My eagerness had blinded me to what, as David pointed out, I ought to have known. 'The fly isn't on the water yet,' he said, 'so the fish won't be feeding. We shall have to wait a bit, I'm afraid.'

I contained my impatience until we set off for Denford to fish some of the Kennet's charming little 'carriers' — the side-streams feeding the main river. The morning dew was still on the meadow-grass; the mayfly were still on the reed stems, waiting for the sun to dry their wings before they could get airborne, and the sky gave promise of a rapturous day. David's labrador, Birdie, with all the faithful patience of its breed, settled into well-behaved repose in the back of his car, obedient, despite the open tail-gate, to his master's firm command. All was right with the Berkshire world.

We set up our tackle and prepared ourselves for the morning ahead. For the first time, I was about to fish the finest chalk-stream in England.* I felt that all my previous angling life had merely been an overture to this moment. Surely Walton had been

---

*I have heard, unbelievingly, that some might dispute this claim, preferring, in their unwisdom, the Test or the Itchen. But they have never enjoyed Mr Channing-Williams's hospitality.

here before me? Surely a dozen generations of country fishermen going back to his days must have felt the same joy in their surroundings as I did?

Like a club golfer teeing off at St Andrews' for the very first time, I was mindful of my historic moment. I had brought with me my favourite rod, a seven-foot C.C. (Casting Club) de France split-bamboo with (I quote from Hardy's Catalogue for 1927), one 'Top Cork-covered Handle, Hardy's Suction Joint, Snake Intermediate, with Agate Butt and End Rings'.

The seven-foot version weighs 3¼ ounces; the eight-foot version, 4¼ ounces, and the nine-foot, which was the original one, 4¾ ounces. The price was a mere £4 18s 6d, not including the 'extras' of 'Screw Grip' Reel Fitting, 'Stud Lock' joints and 'Reversible' Spear and Button, at five, four and seven shillings each respectively. Mine dates from the 1930s and is as straight as the day I bought it second-hand, fifteen years ago. Hardy's had designed it as a tournament casting rod for the great angling competition in Paris, where it was used by one of the brothers. In the typical fashion of the day, the catalogue contained an encomium from a satisfied buyer, one Mr Freeman. He expressed my own views perfectly:–

> I have had the oppportunity of testing the C.C. de France Fly Rod pretty thoroughly, and have nothing but praise for it. I have used it in many awkward places, necessitating an underhand cast and an avoidance of weeds, and have not yet lost a fish once hooked. I have landed fish up to 2lbs and have found this small rod most efficient in its work. It is a most agreeable rod to handle. Its power for such a light tool is remarkable, and I had no difficulty in casting against the wind.

The C.C. de France was designed for casting long distances. It has a stiff dry-fly action which allows the line almost to stop dead in the air, and to drop the fly almost downlike on the water. It is indeed, as Mr Freeman said some sixty years ago, an 'ideal fishing tool', with an action which cannot be bettered by more modern rods in glass, graphite or boron. These may have the right snappy stiffness, but they never quite have the *je ne sais quoi* of a good cane C.C.

Because I felt my rod to be so splendid, I had taken the trouble to dress and waterproof a silk line much finer than any modern synthetic equivalent. With this I knew I should be able to cast both more delicately and more accurately. Such lines were becoming hard to get (I had had mine for several years) but others clearly share my faith in them, since Phoenix Silk Lines have begun to make them again. And although they are priced slightly above the synthetic, the extra cost counts for nought when it is set against fees of perhaps £25 for a day's fishing.

I had been equally selective in assembling the rest of my tackle. I felt the occasion was one which should be lived up to, and had made my preparations accordingly. There is a time for being casual, and a time for being right, and I wanted, as I think most serious fishermen would have wanted, to be right. The pleasure of anything is increased when the tools match and fit the task in hand.

Because I had chosen a silk line, I was able to use a tiny reel: my Hardy (of course) 2½-inch Brass-Faced Perfect, slightly heavier than a modern equivalent, but gleaming with that patina which comes from quality and age and loving ownership. It went perfectly with the rod. So, too, did my fly-box, a beautifully made thing of tortoiseshell-coloured bakelite, with pipe cleaners inside to take dry flies in snug and gentle rows, and my creel, with a Brady bag to take the tackle and a Hardy label on the front to guarantee its workmanship.

The chances of anyone casting a large, bushy fly without occasionally touching vegetation or an old tree stump or bits of fencing post are very slim, so I had also bought a good hook sharpener from Orvis of Stockbridge, an American-owned shop which stocks every angling need under our sun, and probably any other. I always carry it, because to lose a good fish through the sheer carelessness of a dull hook is to do oneself less than justice as a sportsman. It also leaves you feeling very foolish.

Orvis provides a wealth of those other things which fishermen who browse there cannot possibly do without. Or so they tell themselves, despite having done without those things for years. I was seduced by a fly floatant: put the fly into the palm of your hand, powder it lightly and it dries off in an instant. I cannot think how, in my early days, I ever managed without it.

I had the tools, and I was dressed appropriately. It was now time to fish. But for what? The mayfly season is known as 'Duffer's Fortnight', since even the clumsiest beginner can hardly fail to catch something. The fish feed so avidly and carelessly that little art is needed to persuade them to their doom. I wanted something more challenging than a stockie, befuddled by a surfeit of mayflies. What I sought was an observed fish, not one of the mayfly herd.

David is the most thoughtful of fishing hosts. On this occasion he had set me down where two carriers met, about fifty yards from the main river, finding me the best place he knew for my introduction to Kennet fishing. It looked promising, and it was. Almost straightaway, just at the point of the junction, we spotted a large, early-moving brownie of three or four pounds. This, I decided, was to be my fish, and I prepared to go for him; but David, wiser in the ways of the river than I was, counselled caution. So I waited, and watched.

My trout was easy to follow. He pottered about like a gentleman of independent means, contemplating his coming breakfast and wondering what to do with the rest of his watery day. I am not normally anthropomorphic, but the Kennet is that sort of river: sit for a while on its banks and you soon begin to think of Toad and Ratty as real people. And so with my trout: I was almost beginning to feel sorry for him.

There were still only a few mayfly about, and no obvious hatch. Then one or two began to move onto the water. One delicately pirouetted above the waiting lips of my leisured opponent. Languidly he gulped, and the fly disappeared. Now, said David, I could profitably begin to cast.

It was not easy since I was restricted, as previous anglers must have been restricted, by an overhanging willow. It was almost certainly this obstruction which had kept my aquatic aristocrat safe for so long against the intrusion of bourgeois hooks. But not any more. The great advantage of the little C.C. de France was that it allowed me to cast sideways with a short line. And the great advantage of my silk line was that it allowed me to drop my fly with far less disturbance than a heavy synthetic. The odds against the willow tree were rising.

Paradoxically, on so English a river, I was using an American-evolved artificial, the invention of Lee Wulff, a fisherman of many thoughtful parts. He is one of the founders, and a vigorous advocate of, the movement for sporting fishing and had turned his mind not only to flies but to rods. One cane fly rod which he designed for salmon was, incredibly, under two ounces, a weight which cannot be matched even by today's boron rods. It is a six-footer, later made commercially by Sharp under the name of The Midge and I am lucky enough to have one. I use it, very often and very successfully, for Dartmoor trout.

Wulff mainly concentrates on producing big, bushy dry flies, rather like mayflies, for rainbow trout fishing. There is a popular series of them, all with large hackles, wisps for the tail, and robust bodies. They are all easy to tie.

Dry fly fishermen accustomed to fishing the traditional artificial mayfly, greased and dressed in the English way, commonly get them sodden with water very quickly. Wulff's designs have the advantage that they are made from bucktail and various hairs, such as polar bear, which, when they are dressed with water proofing or floatant, allow them to float very high on the water like naturals, with great appeal for the fish.

That morning (after my apologetic time out in praise of Mr Wulff), I was using his Number Ten Grey and feeling very confident. I popped it, rather neatly I thought, just a few feet above my quarry. But he was not to be fooled. He came up, looked at it disdainfully and went back down again, as though it was much too early for that sort of nonsense. He was clearly a Noël Coward sort of trout: Kenneth Grahame would have had him in a velvet dressing gown, smoking a Turkish cigarette out of a long holder, with a Gibson glass in his other hand.

'Don't move it,' warned David. 'Just let it go past and over him. Then lift it off the water very gently from behind him.' I did as I was instructed. On the Kennet, David was my metaphorical Mr

Crabtree, and I was happy to draw on his local knowledge.

I cast again in the same way. Nothing. I tried again. Still nothing. Once more, with skill, but nought to comfort me. At David's suggestion, I brought the fly back and changed it from Grey to Red Wulff. This time, and first cast, it worked: the fish took without a qualm.

I suppose that what happened next took place very quickly. But I saw it as in a movie, when the violent action is suddenly slowed down and filmed slightly out of focus. 'Don't strike!' said David. 'Let him turn on the fly, take the fly down and then just tighten up.'

I was now well and truly into my first big Kennet trout, four shimmering pounds of vibrant energy. He took the whole of the fly-line and the backing and went tearing up the carrier like a rag-raced whippet. He was a fish who had lived for a long time protected by his kindly willow tree, and he had no intention of giving up his comfortable life without a fight. To beat him, I was going to have to employ every scrap of my fishing experience.

Noël Coward was now wide-awake and ready to take on the world. Thankfully, the Brass-Faced Perfect, on which the tension adjuster can be set so that the slightest pull will take the line from the reel, was working well: all I needed to show the fish who was in charge was slight finger pressure on the drum plate. He was still running strongly and had shot up a side-stream, but he came back down when I put pressure on, and I began to think I might have mastered him. My little cane rod was behaving perfectly.

He dived, boring deeply into the water below us. I was sure I had control of him and brought him to the surface, but he was far from beaten. Cocking a cold, fishy eye at me, he suddenly darted off again, speeding down towards the main river, some fifty yards away.

Although I had great faith in the strength of my tackle, there had to be limits to its staying power. I was dealing with a fish which had long lost his early morning langour, and was up and running and displaying a muscled and contemptuous disregard for my angling proficiency. I had no intention of allowing a prized possession to be bent and snapped by a Kennet trout, the cosseted product of a chalk stream. How could a master of Dartmoor's rugged, icy torrents admit to such a humiliation?

I therefore followed him downstream as best I could. I had no real option, however undignified I might have looked to the imposing gentleman fishing from the carefully nurtured and beautifully mown bank opposite me. He watched our progress with some amusement: I doubt if he had ever before seen such an unseemly battle take place off his manicured fastness. His trout probably did as they were told to do.

Mine had no respect for his new and more cultivated surroundings. He continued to struggle and several times leapt like a miniature dolphin, curving the air with silvery grace. Every time he came up I had to drop my rod point to save a breakage, and it must have been fifteen minutes or so before I managed to guide him to the net. Marvelling at his endurance, I administered the *coup de grâce* with my Hardy priest. Nothing less would do.

I laid him on the bank, sparkling against the deep green of the Kennet valley's lush vegetation. David smiled. 'What do you think of fishing on the Kennet, then, Armstrong?' He needed no reply. He knew exactly how I felt. The day was still young, but I had already rated it alpha double plus, and covered my memory of it in bright gold stars. Everything about it had been exactly right.

By mid-morning, the Kennet valley was vibrant with purposeful activity, as full of diverse and bustling life as any inner city. Where we fished was the most rural of places, and the only urban intrusion was the sound of a passing train or occasional motorcycle. But rural cannot be equated with moribund. Wherever one looked, something was happening. The air was thick with humming insects and the sound of bird-song. Coots, moorhens and dabchicks rushed about making their loud alarm calls. Water voles scurried along gravely and somewhere, no doubt, a restless toad was contemplating a change of house. You could hear the summer noise of grasshoppers and crickets and the rippling of the water as fish sucked in passing mayflies. You could watch files of ants passing under a rotting tree root. There were

Gomphus vulgatissimus ×2
"The club tailed dragonfly"
Robin Armstrong '87

A correspondent, David Goddard, told me about this one

Kennet country

Robin Armstrong '87

Scottish Wildcat study
from one of several at
Spakewell, this one always
snarls at me & makes
deep gutteral growls.
Robin Armstrong 19·6·'87

Brown trout

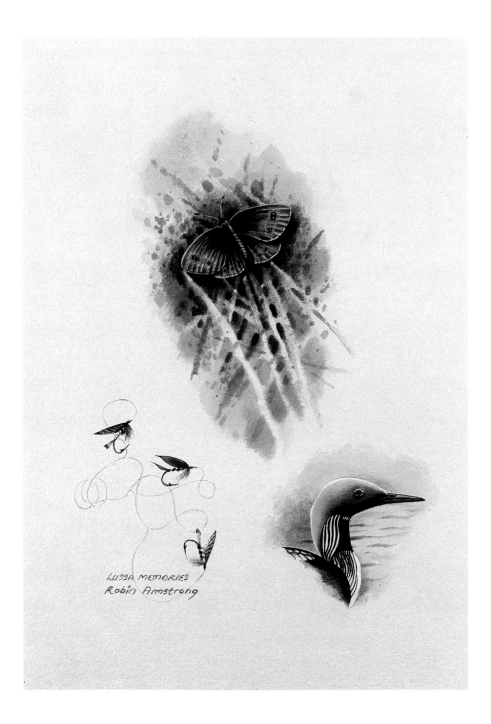

LUSSA MEMORIES
Robin Armstrong

rustlings in the grass and larks wheeling in the sky, and willow warblers doing everything the English Tourist Board could wish of them. Compared with the sometimes inhospitable Devon moors, the Kennet valley was bursting with temperate flora and fauna of every kind.

The roll-call of wild flowers was too long to recite: the names of many were sheer poetry. Ragged Robin, with tiny, purple flowers like small tulips; Devil's Bit Scabious; Marsh Marigold, sometimes known as Mollyblobs, although I don't know why; Red

Marsh marigold

Rattle, delicate and bell-like; *Utricularia Vulgaris*, the Common Bladderwort; and a host of others were within easy sight. Simply to lie on the river-bank and watch what was going on amidst this lush vegetation was enough to engage any man's interest.

We continued to fish that day and we both caught our limit, four apiece I think, but none produced the same thrill as my first. We also caught some grayling from the main river (which pleased Sid, the river-keeper) and generally enjoyed ourselves. It was, quite simply, in the plainest terms I can find to describe it, a blissful day. And until then, I had never realised that anyone could have shared it. The river is not all private water, and permits, given the quality of the fishing, are not expensive. The Kennet may not be open to all, but it is open to those who make a small effort, and for them it will provide a very rewarding return in pleasureable memories.

On my second day, David had to attend his wedding rehearsal. He did so with some reluctance, but even Izaak Walton took time out for marriage, and made up for it by living until he was ninety. Tania was too fine a catch to put at risk, so David left me to my own devices, having kindly arranged for me to have a whole beat to myself.

On my first day at Denford, the river had been slow, deep and moody. Today at Axeford, a mere eight or nine miles away, conditions were totally different. For some inexplicable reason, there are no mayfly beyond Hungerford, and the water was gin-clear and shallow, much more like the Test. Fishing on this stretch, said David, would represent a challenge.

The sun was hot and bright. I would need all my Dartmoor sagacity to achieve anything, but I looked forward to deploying it. When I found a good fish feeding just above some reed beds, I cast as I had done on my first day, just above him, but he ignored me and went down. I had no idea what I had done wrong, and I gnawed at the problem for some time before I realised what had happened. The fault lay not in me but in my fly-box: there was probably nothing in there which this wise old trout had not seen, and rejected, before. Like a good general, I would have to be patient. I would have to wait and observe and analyse my opponent's every move. In particular, I needed to know about his feeding habits. But I was in no hurry. I had the whole day ahead. And I was determined to take him. There was nothing much to see on the water apart from a few small olives, and I had nothing in my fly-box to imitate them exactly. I decided to settle back and see what attracted him.

Nothing happened for about an hour. Then, slowly, he came back and began to feed regularly again. I had already decided I would try him with a Half-Stone which I normally use on my home rivers in Devon, since it sometimes accounts for the 'invisible' food on which a trout seems to be feeding. I gave it a good spray with floatant and tried it out, and then crept back to my pre-chosen casting place. I felt like a marine commando behind enemy lines: one false move and my mission would surely fail.

When a small fly came over him I held my breath. He cocked an eye, looked sideways and then, unhurriedly, took it. I realised that he was used to having all the time in the world to make a close inspection of everything offered to him, whether natural or

Water vole, very numerous on the Kennet

artificial. Compared to my quick-thinking, fast-taking trout on Dartmoor, this judicious old dog was like some canny bureaucrat who had survived every purge by taking no risks whatsoever. He knew the form: very little escaped him. He was going to take a lot of moving.

But a clever trout is still only a trout, and several rungs below Armstrong in the evolutionary pecking order. I was in no doubt that I could outsmart him: I would pit my brain against his piscatorial instincts. I thought that if food were offered to him, his instinct would be to go for it. But if he could see it clearly, all his experience would tell him to give it a second look. So instead of casting above him, where he might see and contemptuously dismiss my pathetic fur-and-feather replica of real food, I decided to put it just beyond his focal, and just behind his full vision. I cast — and truth must take precedence over modesty — little short of perfectly: my fly landed like thistledown, with barely a plop, just behind his nose. He had no time to look at it closely. Instinct told him it was food, and instinct turned him, like a flash, to take it. I was now well into this wise old fish.

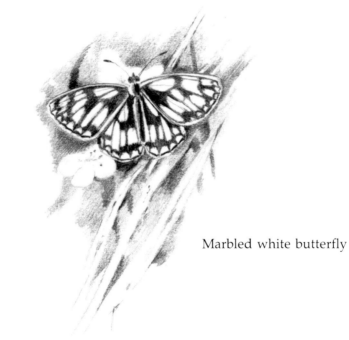

Marbled white butterfly

He fought less hard than I expected. Perhaps he had never before needed to fight: perhaps after a long innings in a well fished river, he fatalistically accepted that his luck had run out. He did dive into his weed bed, and it was not easy, with my light rod to persuade him out. But the resistance was no more than token. Within fifteen minutes he was on the bank. It was time to knock him on the head.

I just couldn't do it. Gleaming in the sunlight, still twitching, he looked too handsome to kill. And having been clever enough to stay uncaught for so long, it seemed unfair not to give him another chance. I felt I had to put him back. Carefully, with a pair of artery forceps, I unhooked him and gently released him into his weed bed. With any luck, protected by his trailing willow, he may be there still.

Sedge warbler — little bird, deafening song

My gesture was not totally sentimental, for I can get as much satisfaction from sparing a worthy opponent as from eating him. When this fish darted away in the summer stream, I knew that I had done the right thing. He deserved his freedom: by giving it, I was able to feel at one both with him and all the other natural life around me.

On a river like the Kennet, which is frequently re-stocked, I shall never move over completely, like most Americans, to catch and release fishing. But if we do not reprieve some of our wild fish, there will very soon be none left to catch. Those who insist on going home every trip with a full creel are hardly true anglers.

I felt no compunction about my next catch. It was a rainbow, hand-reared no doubt, and newly escaped from some nearby fish farm into this hallowed stretch of brownie water. I had no hesitation in marking him down for early despatch into my host's freezer. Even before I caught him, I could tell what he was by the crude way he fed, splashing about at everything which came near him. I took him very easily with a small, dry Green Olive.

After that, I spent most of the rest of my day luxuriating in my lush surroundings, observing the wildlife and making mental sketches for later paintings. Having the place to myself, I felt like the lord of some ancient and especially privileged manor. I wandered the banks, occasionally fished and marvelled at my luck. At lunch-time, I sat in the garden of a nearby pub with my bread, cheese, beer and onions, much as Walton might have done. Surrounded by my rod and reel and the rest of my tackle, I drew some strange looks, but I was immune to them; too drunk with the delights of my day to care what others might think of me.

Since that first visit, I have been back to the Kennet valley almost every year. The contrast with Dartmoor is marked. Where I normally fish, the grass is short and tough; most of the lower hill slopes are covered in bracken and wiry heathers, or reedy bogs and stony outcrops. There are few trees, and the wildlife, inured to hard winters and sparse pickings, is not obvious. The beauty is stark and uncompromising. In the Kennet valley, however, all is soft and green and full of ancient life. Wild flowers grow in profusion. The trees welcome you to accept their shade. At any moment, Puck will emerge from the wood behind the meadow, and Oberon will dance on a sunbeam on the further bank. Wherever you look, something is happening: a dabchick is diving for a tadpole; bees are sucking at willing cowslips; a pike is grabbing for a young duckling. Even in winter, when Dartmoor closes its face to the relentless winds, the Kennet can invite us to fish.

In March 1986 I arrived at David's to become godfather to his daughter. It was the first time I had been asked to fulfill such an honoured role, and fishing was the last thing in my mind.

'I hope you've brought your rod,' said David. I thought he was joking. It was less cold near the Kennet than beside the streams I had just left, but it was still cold. I had not brought my rod. There would be no weed in the river and, as I firmly pointed out to him, the trout would be well out of season and long retired.

'We're not going for trout,' said David. 'We've been asked to take out some pike.'

The surly pike was not a fish I associated with the Kennet, but apparently that placid water contained an unpopular number of them. No keeper wants pike in a trout river, and they needed to be culled.

Equipped with an eight-foot spinning rod borrowed from Tania, I set out with David on the morning of the christening. We caught nineteen fish before lunch, a swingeing haul for someone as conservation-minded as I am. But they had been devastating the trout, and had to be removed.

David caught the biggest, an eleven-pounder taken just beyond the footbridge where Sid, the river-keeper, sat incongruously on a folding garden chair, nursing an appropriately pike-sized hangover. He was trying, without much success, to catch live-bait for us, and rueing his exuberance of the previous evening at the Fishing Club's Annual Dinner.

We fished in what felt like fifteen degrees of frost. Pike are normally said to be tricky to catch, but there was no weed to impede our casting and we needed little skill to take them from the undercut bits of the bank where they lurked. I felt curiously guilty at the ease with which we took fish weighing, on average, about four or five pounds each.

When we got back to the house, our catch was to be discarded. But waste not, want not, I thought, and took them home with me to store in a friend's deep-freeze, since pike is rarely seen in an English fishmonger's. I remembered that the great Izaak, a trencherman of some distinction, had said of stuffed pike that it was 'too good a dish for any but anglers or very honest men'.

I respect his views on these matters as on many others. When I got home, I looked up his recipe. It is too long and complicated to reproduce here, but I commend anyone interested in good food to read it. Suffice it to say that Stuffed Pike à la Walton needs a loving cook, and thyme, and sweet marjoram and a little winter savoury. It needs some oysters and anchovies and sweet butter, and a little mace. And the juice of three or four oranges and claret wine and two cloves of garlic. And a spit, on which to roast it, with care and devotion.

It is a sumptuous dish, and perhaps a fitting one for any feast held in celebration of our English chalk streams. I shall remain true, always, to my Dartmoor Cherrybrook and Cowsic, Walkham and Dart, but all men are entitled to flirt with a second love. I think that if I were ever to be transported, forcibly, to permanent exile in some other clime, the Kennet would be very hard to forget. Whenever June came round, I know I would see the sunlight on that Berkshire water, and hear the varied birdsong, and feel that very special peace of a perfect English summer's day. I might even, treacherously, relish the memory above all others.

A cased brown trout

9

Brown Trout and Red Douggie

Sunday, 5 June, 1977 was a fine, soft West Country morning. I could hear the Walkham rippling its boisterous way down the valley to join its big sister, the Tavy, at Double Waters and I could smell, or perhaps I fancied I could smell, the fresh scent of the untidy trees and bracken which edged its banks and presented casting fishermen with such a challenge. I knew and cherished every feature of that valley; indeed, I knew and cherished every feature of the moor and streams which lay for miles beyond my country door, and I had little mind to leave them, even for a holiday.

But even River Wardens and artists are sometimes distracted from their vocations, and I had recently become bound to another love. I was committed, on that morning, to leave my domain behind to see something of her heritage, while making my peace with the widowed mother from whom I was stealing her. Anne was the girl who had come to outrival fishing for my attention. She was young and shy and very beautiful, with a lilting accent, a smile to melt the iciest of Dartmoor dew-ponds and burnished red hair proclaiming her very Caledonian background. I was determined to marry her and would have walked to Scotland to claim her, if that were necessary.

Anne and I were to be awa', as she would say, by car to the Mull of Kintyre. To Campbeltown, to be precise, a small fishing port serving a hinterland full of rivers and streams rich enough to satisfy the taste of fishermen of every sort.

My own roots were thoroughly English, which is to say they were thoroughly mixed. By ancestry I was Geordie and, in part, Jewish; by birth and upbringing I was Cockney; by adoption I was Devonian. I was also a fisherman and an artist, and to be all these things was to be of the heaven-born. The Scots, I felt, could hardly fail to appreciate me, even though I had only the haziest of notions about them and the place to which we were going.

All my previous knowledge of Scotland came from cinema and television. As far as I was concerned, the Mull of Kintyre could have been some strange laird, like Moncreiffe of that Ilk: I had never thought of it as a promontory to the south-west of Glasgow, jutting out into the top of the Irish Sea. Getting there might prove, from Devon, to be a long, hard drive.

And so it did. It was fifteen hours, with only a short stop for coffee and petrol, before we arrived, tired and dishevelled, at the house of Anne's mother, with me at least surprised by what I had seen on the later stages of the journey. The Mull, which Paul McCartney, who once lived there, described as 'mist rolling in from the sea', was fringed with palm trees and vegetation one normally associates with Torquay. Had I paid more attention at school to my geography teacher, I might have remembered that the Gulf Stream comes straight here from the Spanish coast, bringing welcome warmth to counter the Highland breezes, and allowing chicken-hearts like myself to swim in waters which, without this beneficent infusion, would freeze the warmest marrow.

The drive from Glasgow had been breathtaking. West Devon is lovely enough, and in parts wild and menacing. But it swarms with summer tourists, and it is hardly possible to climb the remotest tor without meeting someone already munching his sandwiches at the top of it. This land was different. It was less crowded. The wild parts were wilder; the spaciousness more evident; the countryside less lived-in and less domesticated. It looked, at first glance, and later proved to be, splendid angling country, with rivers and fish roughly the same as those in the South-West, but with fishermen using very different techniques from those to which I was accustomed.

Female red-breasted merganser

I knew straightaway that it was going to be a good holiday. What fisherman's instinct had led me to a girl who came from such a place? From the very beginning, I felt in sympathy with it. I relaxed. We ate, and we slept, very soundly. And yet I woke unquietly, consumed, as all anglers would be in a place of such potential sport, with the urge to get on to the water as soon as I could decently leave my hostess. By the time he opened, I was already at the friendly door of Mr Armour, the ironmonger, dispenser of mixed nails by the pound, and funny springs for old fashioned door-locks, and other goods never found on the shelves of supermarkets. Mr Armour, I had been told, was the agent for the £2-a-day fishing licences.

'I'm looking forward,' I said, 'to finding some brown trout,' proferring him my money.

'Och!' he answered cheerfully, 'if it's only the brownies you're after, you'll no be needing a licence.'

The fee, I gathered, was only payable by those fishing for salmon and sea-trout: then (and, I think, still) Scotland demands no fee for brownies so long as you get riparian permission.

Business settled, I drove happily along the coast road, past Fort Argyll, to Peninva Bridge. Cars were already parked there, and I could see a small number of worm fishers. The Lussa River, my destination, proved to be much like some rivers in the West Country: perhaps not so fast, nor so bubbly, as the Tavy, but little different — apart from its artificial colour, apparently induced by the discharge of water from the hydro-electric plant on Lussa Loch — from the gentler Oakment in mid-Devon.

The morning was fine enough. I had decided to walk upstream, taking in the countryside as I went, and leaving behind my fellows to their worming. I had already resolved upon taking my brown trout with a fly, but my creel stayed empty. The river may have looked attractive to running salmon and sea-trout, but it was certainly not prolific in brownies.

I meandered on, with little success. Yet the slow walk upstream brought its own rewards. The peace and tranquillity of my surroundings more than compensated for my lack of success. Suddenly, just as I had managed to clear my line from a bankside tree (even River Wardens are permitted some mis-casts), the thicket behind it exploded in a burst of shaken leaves. Out of the top of the tallest tree leapt a very angry and, in its anger, a very beautiful wild cat, spitting and fuming. It hunched, lithely, like the Esso tiger. 'This,' it seemed to say, 'is my demesne. Who are you to intrude upon it?'

In that moment, I was very scared. It was my first sighting of this rare, primordial creature in its native habitat, although this must surely have been the most southerly point in its range. I was torn between delight at seeing it and real terror that it might attack me. But it disappeared almost as quickly, if much more silently, than it had arrived, slinking away with all the 'fearful symmetry' of all untamed felines. I felt very privileged to have seen it.

My euphoria didn't last. Back at my car, two large, red-faced Highlanders awaited me. 'Your licence, if you please,' said one of them, with the air of a man who already knew he was going to get an unsatisfactory answer.

'No licence,' I replied, confident in Mr Armour's assurance that I hadn't needed one. 'I was only after the brownies.'

'Oh aye?' said my interrogator, with all the disapproval of a John Laurie addressing Captain Mainwaring. 'There are nay brownies in this water, so I'll just be troubling you for the two pounds.'

Both men were by now beginning to look even larger than when I first saw them. I tried to explain. Showing them my River Warden's warrant card, with my work number, 1974, and the picture of a man whom, I had to admit, looked rather sprucer and spritelier than I now did, I asked them, 'Would I, a River Warden in Devon, try to escape paying the proper dues?'

They evidently thought I would. 'Ye may have been a bailiff in 1974,' said the one I had (very silently) christened Big MacDonald, 'but that does'na mean you're one noo.'

I paid the two pounds. Not of course lest he turn me upside down with one hand while he shook the money out of my pockets with the other, but simply because I didn't want to make a fuss. And anyway, it wasn't often I was able to make giants smile.

Perhaps it was standard form to catch all visitors in this way. Certainly the local constabulary confirmed later that the river had few or no brownies in it, even though Mr Armour had been right in saying I didn't need a licence for them.

The Lussa never did become my favourite river. I learned to prefer Carradale Water, the river which flowed eastwards through the upland forest to Carradale itself, a tiny seaport some fourteen miles north of Campbeltown. Carradale was typical of many small fishing places, but with a community even more tightly knit than most. The people were hardy and hard-working, living thrifty lives centred on the slightly old-fashioned, but sturdy and workmanlike clinker-built boats which then cluttered the harbour. Nowadays, heavier and bigger steel Norwegian trawlers predominate, and the traditional designs are steadily being phased out.

To hear the powerful diesels of a fifty-foot trawler starting up ready to move off, stirs the blood˙of all but the most confirmed land-lubber. And to watch the boats, as they sail across the bar, causes many a clerkly holiday-maker to wish he, too, did something less pedestrian for a living. Most of us, I suppose, take a romantic view of those who go down to the sea in ships, especially small ships, but in truth of course, the men of Campbeltown and Carradale, and the 'Easties' of the Ayrshire coast, led lives which for the most part were harsh and arduous.

Carradale trawler waiting for the evening tide

Fishing for prawn by day and herring by night was not a job for faint hearts. Rivalry between boats was intense: the work was always demanding and, though occasional catches brought large rewards, it was an uncertain life. Bad weather could interrupt sailings, and the upkeep of boats and gear was expensive, for fishermen, like farmers, are constantly having to improve their technology.

In the end, it is still the skipper's gut-feelings, his skills and experience in measuring the ways of wind and weather, and his luck which count for more than all the modern sonars and radars in bringing home a good catch. His job is not one to be learned at college. It demands the deployment of a keen judgement which can only be honed by long experience. For a young man, the best classroom was the heaving deck of a trawler, and the only way to learn was to watch and listen to those, probably from your own family, who had done the job for years before you.

On that first visit north, I fixed, as bold (or foolhardy) visitors could, to go out on one of these boats. And fascinated by the skills of Jimmy MacDonald, my first guide, I have continued to go out with him ever since. Jimmy, known as Jimmy Noon to distinguish him from his father, was a Campbeltown man, and a fisherman born and bred. As soon as he legally could, and no doubt before that, he was off to learn his life's trade from his father. But he had too much drive and intelligence to remain a crew boy. In time he became his own man with his own boat: equal partner with his father in the tricky business of pair-trawling.

That was later. When I first knew him he was crewing, and another wise old skipper, the canny and sagacious Cecil (pronounced, incongruously, Ceecil) Finn, was pairing with Jim's father's boat; he plied his ancient trade with great ingenuity and resource. And in pair-trawling these qualities are essential to success.

In outline, 'pair-trawling' was done by suspending a net between two boats and dragging it along at a pre-fixed level to scoop up herring. The technique demanded all the skipper's concentration, since any marked divergence from the agreed course could split the net or drag it through the water at a quite unproductive depth.

I looked forward to my first night on a small trawler. I knew the weather would not bother me. I was used to working in the dark and in the rain, and I rarely felt the cold. But what I forgot was that River Wardens have their feet firmly anchored to unmoving ground or, at worst, to the bed of a stream. Trawlermen have to survive on a deck which is never still, which rolls and pitches constantly even in the calmest of seas.

That realisation only dawned later. For the moment, I was on the quay with some others, keenly anticipating the new experience ahead. We tried to look nonchalant. The crew began to arrive in dribs and drabs. No one spoke much. Men simply got on with their various tasks, going through the well-established procedures of getting ready for sea. It was obvious that every man knew exactly what was required of him.

I thought I was good on boats and ships. I had travelled on everything from small launches in Plymouth Sound to ocean liners, and I had never been sick. But this, after we had left the harbour, was different. Trawlers roll and pitch and heave and sway and corkscrew like no other sea-going vessels. By 2am I not only felt physically unwell, but claustrophobic, paranoid and ready for some easeful death. I was trapped in this tiny craft in the middle of a large sea and I wanted to get off. This kind of fishing, I decided, was a mite different from standing on a pleasant river bank, trying to out-think an elusive trout in the pool below: this was work, and cruelly hard work at that, not pleasure.

'You're not looking so well,' said Jimmy, with typical Highland meoisis. 'Shall we go below for a bite to eat? That'll cheer ye up no end.' I accepted his invitation. When I climbed down the small hatch, I found that 'below' was a tiny cabin, thick with the smell of diesel fumes and sweaty socks, and shuddering with the constant vibration of the powerful engine in the forward hold. It was no rest room: the stink, made worse by the greasy smells wafting from the cooking stove, and the noisy thumping of the engine, did nothing to improve my condition.

I should not have enlisted, I thought. Here, in this cramped and foetid hell-hole, I shall quietly and ingloriously expire. '*Hic jaecet* Armstrong,' they will write on my headstone, 'Died at sea of malignant odours to the gentle sound of a Volvo Penta and the rumblings of his ravaged insides.'

In my distress, I regarded the appearance of the cheerful crewboy without enthusiasm. He brought with him a steaming potful of ghastly-looking, greyish mince and a loaf of rubbery,

Heron

off-white bread. Removing a somewhat battered ladle from his back-pocket, he wiped the business-end across his grimy trousers and proceeded to scoop large blobs of the awful mince into the cereal bowls which sat insecurely on the swaying table.

I swallowed, with difficulty. But the breakfast was not complete. He had yet to place a poached egg on the top of each pile of meat, to lie there, yellow, white and unwinking, like the eye of a giant sheep at a pagan feast.

It was too much. I left the cabin and groped for the fresh air, thinking I was the victim of some atavistic west coast conspiracy, a rough joke played on all newcomers, by mariners whose roots stretched back beyond known history. But I was wrong. The mince and poached egg were standard sea-going fare. 'It's a real delicacy,' said Jimmy, 'a real delicacy, though ye may not think so. It's funny old ways we have up here.'

And so they were, funny old ways. Later, when my mind had cleared and I was beginning to feel human once more, I had the glimmering of a memory that I had heard of minced beef on toast, with poached egg, somewhere before. I looked it up. Sure enough, it was in Mrs Beeton: presumably a standard part of that stern nursery diet which sustained the Empire-builders in the time of the old Queen. For my own part, were I a full-time trawlerman, I think I might look for a somewhat less intimidating breakfast.

Back on deck, I had recovered my poise. I even managed, hungry by this time, to eat some mince. The hair of the dog, so to speak, cured me: I was better, and soon enjoying myself. And the experience, which I was to repeat on many occasions, helped me also to understand the character of those fishermen I was to meet ashore. Almost all of them were friendly and helpful; almost all of them were prepared to share their knowledge and experience with this English stranger. When there is no great pressure on the available water, fishermen can afford to be magnanimous. It is only in the crowded south that they sometimes forget the common courtesies.

Mr Martindale was the old man, in his seventies, who gave me my permit to fish Carradale Water from Gamekeeper's House on

In All His Glory

the Carradale estate of Naomi Mitchison, novelist and veteran socialist. The place had a strong family and community feel about it: one felt immediately at home there. Fishing was let out by the day, and Mr Martindale dispensed free advice as well as licences. 'Wait for the spate,' he said, 'then fish hard and wait for the next spate.' This, I recalled, was much as one fished the Dart, 500 miles to the south, and I relished the sport which awaited me.

The Carradale seemed to be empty of fellow-anglers apart from one wild one, a woolly-looking man with hair the colour of a polished pillar-box. As was common, he was using a worm and, as I approached, he struck, swiftly and efficiently. He continued to play what was obviously a big fish with an easy, deceptively casual skill. He was clearly a master of his craft: practised and economical in his movements, and articulating the clutch on his reel with a confidence which I envied. It wasn't long before a magnificent gleaming ten-pound salmon lay beside him on the beach at the side of the pool.

Before I could offer him my congratulations, he produced a bottle of whisky from one of his capacious pockets. It was apparent, from the smell on his breath, that some of the precious liquid had already passed his lips earlier that morning. But not, clearly, in the quantity he needed. Lifting the bottle, he took a swig which, on any Richter scale of liquor drinking would have rated at least nine, and then turned to me. The drink seemed not to have affected him, although, in truth, neither his bright red hair nor his leathered face could have got any redder than they already were.

I muttered my praises and admiration. 'Aye, aye,' he said, accepting my words as no more than his proper due. 'Are ye from round these parts?'

I was not, I said. I came from England. 'Then ye'll know nothing about fishing in the Carradale?'

I forebore to say that I knew the Dart, and that from the advice given me by Mr Martindale the rivers might be the same. I contented myself with telling him that friends had told me where the likely pools might be found.

'Och,' he said, 'take no account of them. Just follow me and you'll soon see how to catch fish.'

And I did. In the next half hour, he caught three specimens any one of which would have delighted a Devonian heart. I was clearly in the presence of a local genius: a primitive piscatorial god of highland streams; a genuine natural fisherman.

I introduced myself. I didn't catch his name, but I didn't need it. Everyone, he said, called him Red Douggie, and he'd be happy to share a dram with me at any time.

Later in the week, I asked Jimmy Noon about him. 'Red Douggie, was it?' he exclaimed. 'Ay, he's verra well known. He's a nice man, but a real nutter.'

'Is that because of all the whisky he puts away?' I asked.

'Och, no, no, no!' he denied the thought. 'He's as mad without the whisky as he is when he's majestic.'

I savoured the word. As Jimmy said it, in all the glory of his rich brogue, I thought how marvellously it fitted Red Douggie. It matched him perfectly, for I could never imagine him out of control, drunk or sober. The way he handled a rod told me that. Far more likely that the whisky, however much he drank of it, would merely enlarge him and make him more splendid than he already was.

Jimmy told me that Red Douggie was a master crewman on the trawlers. This paid for the whisky which Douggie drank almost continuously. But for a man in his mid-forties, he was surprisingly spry. Once, said Jimmy, the boats had been fleeing back to port to escape a sudden and fearful tumult which had blown up from nothing. They had been trawling for ground fish, and the nets were out when the storm caught them. All the boats turned back, with the Carradale boats passing those from Campbeltown on their way to their home port. Jimmy's boat veered towards a large metal trawler. He could hardly see over the bows for mist and spray. Suddenly, out of the murk, he came sideways on to the other vessel. Between the squalls, he saw a wild apparition hanging over the stern of the other boat, trying to free an entangled net. It was Douggie: mad, maybe, but a skilled and valuable hand. Only he would have taken such chances in such vile conditions.

I spent many happy hours with Douggie, and learned a lot

from him. His methods, so productive, had obviously developed from long and wide experience. Usually he favoured an eight- or nine-foot spinning rod with a fixed spool reel and a small, drilled bullet. He had a 15lb mono filament line, and fished the pools by casting upstream, feeding the worms back to him rather than ledgering, in rather boring fashion, downstream. It was an interesting, 'heavy duty' version of the upstream worming which I have practised in the South-West, and it was based on sheer efficiency and knowledge.

Douggie, although in appearance and outward character he was hardly the type to do so, stuck rigidly to the proper rules. He would fish with a fly when the conditions were right and with the worm when the rivers were in spate. But until he had passed

Grey seal — Sealpoint, Kintyre

the village where it was permitted, he would never use his spinner: despite his eccentricities, he stayed within the laws of the river and the conditions imposed by the owners. The energy and power of his fishing was immense. He could catch salmon or trout with equal facility by all three methods.

Loch fishing on the Mull was second to none, and on a different scale to similar fishing in the South-West. Lussa Loch, for example, was about the same size — some seventy or eighty acres — as Fernworthy Reservoir, near Chagford. But its surrounds were less tame and richer in wild life. There were fewer people about, and naturalists could enjoy the sight of birds and butterflies in peace and serenity. But not without noise. Sitting there or standing, walking the river or the bank, or just lying on the grass and watching the clouds, one rarely escaped the weird mewings of the red-throated divers which scanned the water's edge for things to eat. Loons, I think the Americans call them, perhaps because of their distinctive wailings, likened once, to 'the hoarse voice of a woman crying out in agony.'

On the moors beyond the loch, there were also lots of hen harriers. Forty years ago they were rarely seen outside the Orkneys and the Outer Hebrides. Now they were commonplace. More rare, although I spotted it often enough during those high summer afternoons, was the peregrine falcon, waiting to dive (at a hundred or more miles an hour, or so they say) at some loitering pigeon or unsuspecting rabbit. And once, and gloriously, I watched a golden eagle, huge wings spreading over seven feet from tip to tip, fly majestically over my deserted hillside. There cannot be many people who have shared the sight of this King of the Highlands. It has been known, occasionally, to take small lambs. Seeing it in flight, it looked capable of tackling a fully grown lamb; or even, perhaps, some two-legged intruder into its private killing grounds.

Over the years, I learned to be protective of these hills and rivers. Once, when a four-wheel drive vehicle came charging over the moor, filled with a group of excited Germans, I felt a great desire to protect and defend the privacy of the local community. 'Where,' asked the Germans, stopping with a screech of tyres, 'do the Paul McCartneys live?' The McCartneys were no part of my world and I had never met them, although I knew where they lived. Uncharacteristically, I heard myself say, 'I know where they live, but I'm afraid I can't tell you.' Afterwards, when I thought about it, I realised that I was unconsciously slipping into the ways of my hosts. I was beginning to become one of them: polite, but reserved, as jealous for the privacy of others as for my own.

During that first holiday, and later, I spent many hours on Lussa Loch, all of them enjoyable. I could catch brown trout there at almost any time, so long as they were on the feed. Indeed it was not unusual to use a dropper of three flies and to have a couple of fish 'on' at the same time. Normally I would use a nine-foot cane rod with a number five weight, forward line and two traditional flies, Mallard and Claret, plus perhaps one other such as Black and Peacock Spider. They never failed me. Nor did I ever tire of the birds and the scenery and the changing skies. On misty or rainy days I fished hard. Often, when it was fine, I would simply lie on the tough grass and count the blessings of a sporting and artistic life. I could return home to my mother-in-law's knowing that there was always tomorrow, and more fishing, and maybe even a pint or two of Scottish ale in a local pub to set the seal on a halcyon day.

Anne's mother lives in one of a group of four flats on the road out of Campbeltown towards the RAF base. Our relationship, at first, was tentative and wary on both sides. She belonged to that strict branch of northern protestantism which regards most sorts of frivolous pleasure with deep suspicion. Fishing, I think, was not positively damned in her eyes, but it did provide large numbers of unreliable husbands with an excuse to leave home during the dreaded Opening Hours, and it therefore had to be viewed carefully. It also cost money which might be better 'saved for a rainy day'.

Fishermen are not very upset by rainy days: in fact, they often welcome them. I reached an understanding with my mother-in-law that I would not comment on her beliefs if she would forego criticism of mine. We did, after all, both love the same person, and after a while we both agreed that to live and let live was no bad prescription for happy lives.

Our unspoken compact came under strain almost as soon as it was made. One grey day I had left the flat after lunch and rushed past her neighbour, Malcolm MacMillan, to my car. In our new-found amity, my mother-in-law had come to the balcony to see me off. I looked up. She waved, and I, replete with luncheon and goodwill, waved back, slamming the car into gear and driving off at the same time. The fates were unkind. The car shot backwards with rare verve, straight into mama's brand-new-that-morning, hot-from-the-dealer's hand, still-showroom-gleaming Peugeot.

Strict Christians may spurn both the pleasure of the flesh and the pleasures of possessions. But we all have weaknesses, and the Peugeot was hers. As is the way of such things, I damaged the new car considerably more than I damaged my old one.

I wound down the window and sought support from Mr MacMillan.* He knew my mother-in-law well, and was having no part in this débacle. Shaking his head, perhaps more at the universal follies of mankind than at this particular manifestation of them, he looked at me sadly and said, 'You're for it noo, laddie, you're for it noo!' and departed, slamming his door behind him.

There is a gloom in all Scottish prophecy from Cawdor onwards which chills the spirit. I doubt if any Highland seer has ever foretold joy rather than woe. From then onwards, my ability to handle things mechanical has remained in doubt, at least in the cold eye of the Peugeot-owner: artists, and people who stand in the rain catching things, often only to put them back, are not to be trusted in the same way as Town Hall Men, and Bank Men and Men who Work for Reputable Insurance Companies.

I arranged for the cars to be repaired and drove off to the never-failing comfort of Lussa Loch. There, of all the priests in all the world, I met my mother-in-law's Minister. Belying her puritanism, he proved to be a fishing enthusiast. I learned from him that, for sea-trout and salmon, one could fish from the rocks above Carradale, straight into the sea. 'Listen for the cries of gulls or terns,' he said. 'The birds will provide a sure guide to the shoal of fish. Then fish as hard as you can.' I did as he said, and proved his advice to be sound. I also enjoyed being on the rocks of a coast which teemed with bird life.

Prawn-fishing with Jimmy Noon off Ailsa Craig, a great chunk of volcanic rock rising some 1100 feet out of the Firth of Clyde, I watched thousands of great, greedy gannets, swooping and

---

*Mr Macmillan was a stick-maker and retired shepherd. His son Archie gave me a beautiful and useful traditional Scottish crook. 'If ye ever break it over the back of a poacher,' he said — for like me, he had no illusions about the villainy of the gangs who were prepared to wreck the ecology of rivers for gain — 'I'll replace it for free'. The offer has not yet had to be redeemed. Sadly, Archie died last year.

Gannet — thousands of them in Kintyre

wheeling above their breeding cliffs, dive-bombing their target fish with breathtaking precision. Apart perhaps from Bass Rock in the Forth, the gannetry on Ailsa Craig must be the most famous in Britain. It is a living island of birds, stinking, even from way out at sea, of the ammonia spawned by its thousands of peripatetic and voracious visitors. Local fishermen take the gannets for granted: to a stranger, the sight of them in such numbers is unforgettable.

Gigha Island was also memorable, but for different reasons. Here the Gulf Stream had created a benevolent mini-climate, moist and warm, in which sub-tropical plants, in a garden at Achamore House, flowered in profusion. The loch-fishing there

Sunset over Gigha

provided brown trout — true brownies, not stocked fish — even bigger and more succulent than those on the Mull. The place was an altogether surprising paradise of rich agriculture and bird life in waters which paradise-seekers would not normally explore. There were no sand flies on the beaches; the sea was crystal-clear, and small, prolific lochs, packed with trout, abounded.

That first holiday was a revelation. The Mull, and the waters on it and around it, afforded me fishing as fine as I have ever known. I caught brown trout; rainbow trout (in the warm waters from the power station); sea trout, and the salmon itself. I caught cod, sea-fishing off the Clyde, and mackerel (which the local people considered to be vermin, but they're nice eating, very fresh, despite that) and, above all, I had caught for me, mainly by Jimmy, prawns; delicious, Dublin Bay 'hale' (whole) prawns.

'Take your feed of prawns hame with ye,' Jimmy would say, at the end of a tiring but deeply fulfilling day on his boat, scooping up a 'feed of prawns' fit for an emperor. And I felt like an emperor, without his pomp and responsible circumstances. To be able to fish, and paint, and walk the rivers and sail the sea, and then come home to bright-cheeked Anne, was more, I felt, than any man could wish for.

10

Fresh Salmon

More books have been written about salmon than about any other fish. That, at least, is my suspicion, and when I am old and grey and arthritic, and can no longer fish, I shall visit the British Library to confirm it.

But even if I am proved wrong, only those who go down to the waters off Miami, in search of barracuda and other monsters, would deny salmon's first place on the angler's list of desirable catches. It is a fish of mystery and of majesty: mystery, because no one fully understands its unique life cycle; and majesty, because it is a good-looking, regal fish, well-proportioned and gleaming, full of grace and power in the water and replete with gastronomic promise when it is finally landed and cooked. It provides both good sport and good eating; pleasure both to those who chase it and to those non-fishermen to whom it is borne home in triumph.

I shall not dwell on the puzzle of its peregrinations from the headwaters of tiny rivers like the Walkham and the Tavy, out into the depths of the great Atlantic and back to its home waters. Why and, just as important, how a fish should choose to roam so far and then return, of all the rivers in all the world, to the one in which it was spawned, is not fully understood. But even if it were, and the light dawned, and we ceased to view their fabled journeyings through a glass darkly, the romance would remain. I should continue to marvel at the sureness of a salmon's instincts, and to delight in the sight of it leaping its determined way up the brawling streams of late spring. Of all the river's pictures, none can match that of a salmon, creating its own small rainbow as it arches up and over a sunlit rapid.

Salmon is rarely out of the angling headlines. People fight over it; go to gaol over it; and sometimes lose their lives in pursuit of it. Among fishermen, it excites envy: among poachers, it generates greed. And understandably, for in Tavistock alone one man may take as many as thirty illegal fish a week. Over twenty-five weeks of the year, this represents a substantial sum of untaxed income, for which villains are prepared to run many risks — and to offer, on occasion, much violence to those who dare to stand between them and the prizes they seek. Every river-keeper must learn to live with the constant malignity of the gangs from whom he tries to protect his expensive charges.

The honest poacher, true to the virtues of good fishing practice, and steadfastly removing no more than his immediate needs, is a corrupt fiction; a myth created by magazine writers, or by poachers themselves perhaps, when they appear in court, bland and fawning. In practice, most of them are highly organised, well-equipped and ruthless. They are neither poor nor honest nor blessed with hearts of gold. Quite simply, they are rogues, short-sighted in their pursuit of immediate gain, and mostly unpleasant. Left to their greedy selves for two seasons, they would destroy salmon-fishing in Britain for ever. In four words, I love them not.

Everyone who has ever wielded a successful salmon rod on only a few occasions believes himself a salmon expert. Let him do so ten times and he will want to write a book describing his experiences, and I can understand that. It is the way of those finding a new love to imagine that none before them has ever known the ecstasy they have freshly enjoyed. It is therefore possible to find a thousand volumes about salmon-fishing, all of them good, so there is little point in my adding to the literature. What follows are merely a few reflections on this handsome fish, and some of the handsome people who fish for it, rather than a set of instructions in technique. For a proper text-book, seek elsewhere.

The best salmon man I know is David Channing-Williams, whose hospitality I have already recounted. Most of his days are spent at a desk, helping to run a large company. Time is precious to him and, when he fishes, he applies himself totally to his task. And this, I think, is the secret of his fishing success — or perhaps of all success. Channing-Williams works for his angling rewards. He is thorough; he observes his fish; he studies every stone and quirk of the river he fishes; he watches the weather and the state of the water and, if it were relevant, he would study the ways of every minnow in the river. His commitment is awe-inspiring.

Anyone (almost) can fish the rich and lush wide rivers of Scotland, with a wise gillie on hand to tell you where to place and how to level your double-handed rod, in order to haul in some fat catch. But the capricious, rock-filled, tricky, peat-stained waters of the South-West are a different matter. You must be skilled and sure-footed and wise to its moods to work a stream with any success: you must be prepared to search every single inch of water before you give up. Salmon will lie anywhere they can find a good, well-aerated position, and it was David who taught me that if their historic lies are empty, then they are not necessarily unfindable.

I had first met him when he was well into a fourteen-pound salmon. This, I learned later, was his sixth of the week. It was downstream of him, a position in which, he later instructed me, no fish should ever be. For once, his quarry had got the better of him: Homer had nodded.

The art of playing a salmon is akin to the art of catching one. You need sagacity; you need to keep your head; above all, you need courage to slacken your line when the fish of a lifetime is going seawards. Every instinct will tell you to exert pressure on the fish. But if you do, and your salmon wants to go in the other direction, then you will lose it. You have to give him his head. But you must also know when and how much check to apply to your fleeing quarry.

This time, David was lucky. The fish was 'fresh-run', in on the tide (it still had sea-lice on it) and weary from its long battle upstream, for Grenofen, where we were, was some fourteen miles upstream from the estuary, near Tavistock. I lent him a bailiff's hand. Getting behind the rock where the fish was lodged, I netted it for my new-found acquaintance and began a friendship which I still cherish.

I say that David was lucky that his fish did not escape, but that is true only in part, for good fishermen make their own luck. Admittedly, on those very rare occasions when we are cursing our lack of rain, he has only to start driving west for the heavens to open and the rivers to fill. But that is not luck: it is simply the Lords of the Angle rewarding him for his long and devoted service to their cause.

Fish are attracted to David like iron filings to a positive charge, perhaps because that is how he thinks. He is a master-fisherman: the kind who attracts good fortune by hard work and skill; who deserves success because he earns it. If he catches fish when others fail, it is because he concentrates harder than they do, and never misses a potential chance, however slender.

Do salmon sense his presence and give themselves up, I wonder, knowing they have little chance against his determined pursuit? I am never sure. But I am sure that his speed of action, his confidence and his thoroughness are the qualities needed by every angler who seeks success.

On the Walkham, in the good river conditions which follow a big spate, the usual method is to spin, in the traditional way, across and downstream, so that the spinner comes round in the flow and presents an attractive target for the fish. Using this basic technique, you should then vary your approach according to different conditions. Early in the season, your bait will need to be suspended lower in the water than in high summer, when the

Toby lure — good early season bait

fish come nearer the surface. At other times, you will simply want to flit it invitingly across the tail of the pool.

David would vary the angle of his spinner to suit every case, fishing almost as he would with a fly; an eight- or nine-foot rod in his right hand; a bunch of line in his left, and the spinner angled and dangled as he wanted it. On a relatively narrow river, he covers most of the water without any need to cast, and when a fish takes, he is able to slacken off for a brief second before really connecting.

This is important, for most salmon take and turn almost simultaneously, and many are lost as they do so, especially when the bait is a spinner. As the fish grabs, the angler's immediate instinct is to strike straightaway, but if he does this, then nine times out of ten the hook will come straight out, particularly if the fish is downstream. Resolve, therefore, to be brave: give your salmon the chance to turn before you strike and thereby give yourself the chance to hook it in the maxillary bone where a salmon is most likely to stay hooked.

The upper reaches of the Walkham call for nothing but straightforward fishing and fitness. It is no river for the decrepit, nor for those who expect to stay in one small reach. You need to fish a long stretch, and methodically. You need a rod long enough to cover water which is rarely wider than ten feet, and tough enough to withstand the rushes of a fish over harsh granite rocks. For a fly, follow the advice which the locals give me and use 'zummat with a bit of orange in it'. The colour is more important than the shape.

You can also get good results with worms, but you will need to exercise more skill and diligence than if you were fishing, say, the placid waters of a Scottish loch. Unless you search the river unceasingly, and work the pots and guts behind every rock, you will probably find nothing. The one place you carelessly miss may be just the one which harbours your potential catch.

Finally, and perhaps above all, you must remember that no human has senses more alert than those of a wild creature. By the time you see a salmon, the chances are that it has already seen you. So leave it in peace, and move on to find another fish: whatever you offer by way of bait, the fish which is aware of your alien presence is unlikely to accept it.

On Dartmoor rivers, moving on can sometimes be hazardous: in spate, they carry an intimidating amount of fast-flowing water, and only the expert should take risks with them in such conditions. I thought, after ten years in the South-West, that I was such an expert. Until, that is, I went out on the Dart with a local man who had known the river all his life.

Spindle Easterbrook is a Prison Officer at Her Majesty's Prison, Dartmoor, and I suppose that fishing provides a very welcome relaxation from the rigours of his duties in that forbidding granite fortress. Like David Channing-Williams, and perhaps all the best anglers, he is generous in sharing his knowledge and experience: I always enjoy being with him. On this occasion, we were exploring the Dart when he spotted a fish dimpling and sheering on the opposite bank. The river was in full spate, bubbling down over the rocks in great spurts of white water. I saw no way we could get to the fish.

Spindle was not deterred. 'Right, boyo,' he said, 'let's go across and have a look at it,' and promptly stepped out into the water. I expected him to sink up to his thighs, for the river looked deep: in parts, I knew it to be over twenty feet. But he, of course, knew every stone, even those hidden below the rushing current. 'Follow me!' he commanded, and I did. But I would not have followed anyone else.

Few of us, including water-bailiffs, can ever presume to know a river as well as that. But to fish well in the west country, you do need to empathise with both your surroundings and the fish you hope to catch. Just as a successful Master of Hounds knows intimately the country over which he hunts and the habits of the fox which is his quarry, so do the best fishermen know their own rivers and the ways of the fish within them. Local men like Roy Buckingham, Dave Pilkington, Gilly Warne (a cousin of Fernley) and Dave French seem to know almost from hour to hour where the fish may be found. Glyn Lloyd-Jones claims he can even tell which river a salmon comes from, and perhaps he can, although I cannot. To my eye, no two salmon are alike. All I can distinguish is an especially long, lean type with a large tail which runs mainly in the Tamar and is therefore known locally as a Tamar Greyhound.

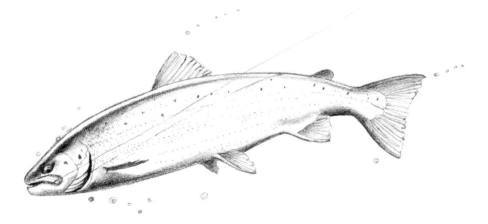

First plunge for freedom — Tamar Greyhound

By the time I took my first salmon, on the Walkham near Grenofen, I was an experienced fisherman. But a salmon was different, and more difficult than anything I had known before: I knew nothing about playing the fish, and simply hung on to it as best I could. What I had been looking at were brown trout, and it was only by chance that, when the salmon appeared, I had a bigger rod in my car, and a bigger fly. Once I had hooked the fish, my instinct was not to let go. Fortunately, Grenofen Pool is an accommodating place. And fortunately, the fish decided to go upstream, towards the weir, instead of down. At the point where the water narrowed into a small stickle, rushing through at speed, I was able to exert some pressure and control it.

My salmon, which I finally landed more by good luck than good management, was just over nine pounds of sparkling spring flesh, covered in sea-lice, but otherwise a fine sight. After I had killed it, I laid it on the bank beside my rods, trying to control my excitement. The composition was perfect, but my audience — of which I had been unaware — was not impressed. Sitting on the bridge, swinging their legs over the parapet, were four of Tavistock's most notorious poachers. I somehow doubted that they shared my aesthetic pleasure in the scene I had unwittingly created for them.

Since then I have taken salmon, and not a few poachers, every year. I have learned that catching a salmon, whoever does it and wherever it is done, by a small boy on the Tavy or a laird on the Tay, is always an event. Everyone stops to watch it being played and landed: everyone crowds round afterwards to admire it. I have also learned that salmon provides supreme sport. The only British fish which comes close to it in bodily power is the carp, on its first screaming run, or perhaps the bass, in the shallow waters of an estuary. I have heard, too, that bone fish and similar species, caught in salt-water mud flats, are hard to stop. But the fighting prowess of a big salmon cannot be equalled, not only in the pursuit but in the landing. You have only won your battle when it is safely lying on the bank.

Every salmon man has his own foibles and cherishes his own faiths. One of mine is to believe that the first essential of success lies in keeping calm. If you fear that you are about to lose your fish, then that fear will be transmitted down your line and give your catch the confidence to outwit you. A salmon, after all, can navigate, inexplicably, over vast distances: why should it not sense a weakness in the opponent who seeks to capture it? There are more things in heaven, and in the waters of upper Dartmoor, than any scientist can possibly explain.

Once you have hooked it, exert the maximum possible pressure on your fish, but in the nicest possible way. Brutality is to be avoided: simply let the fish know, politely but firmly, that you are in control. Do not let it go downstream, at least on rivers in the South-West, otherwise you may lose your battle before it has really begun. A salmon will use the rush of water at the pool's throat to carry it downstream, where there will almost certainly be rocks and trees waiting to snag and saw away even lines of ten– twelve pounds' breaking strain, leaving you bereft and fishless.

I have read, although I cannot remember where, that a salmon will fight for one minute for every pound of its weight. Allow, therefore, ten minutes of struggle with a ten-pounder, but do not be surprised if you take less, or need more time, than this: the rule, in my experience, is far from absolute, and salmon are rarely amenable to neat categorisation.

In rivers which are deep and wide and sensible, you may relax very slightly, for you will have ample space in which to work. But in West Devon, eternal vigilance must be the price of your success. Once you have hooked your salmon, be at once cautious and bold: bold enough to exert the pressure which tells it who is master, but cautious enough not to overplay your stern hand and so lose it. The line to be drawn is fine, and the road to glory demands both brains and bravery. One without the other is not enough.

Even now your work is not over. A salmon, however hard you have fought it, is still capable of one final, explosive, escaping burst of energy. Much care is still needed to land him, for few fishing experiences are more upsetting than that of playing a fish for fifteen or twenty minutes and then having it break free at the last moment, perhaps with a lure or a fly still in its mouth.

In some rivers, you can simply beach your fish by walking him backwards and leading him, gently but firmly, to the resting place you have chosen for him. But first find your beach: on most rivers in the South-West, you would have to search long and hard before you found anything remotely suitable. You are therefore left with gaffing, tailing or netting, and of these, I always favour the last.

Gaffing in this region is illegal at certain times: and tailing is too often ineffective, since it is difficult to re-set a tailer, if you miss first time, when your other arm is attached to a rod with a lively salmon on the end. I therefore opt for a guy net which slides up and down a central pole, and which fits by way of a convenient peel sling, allowing it to be pulled and released instantly onto the bank beside you, ready for action. It requires some manipulative skill, but of all the ways of finally getting your salmon into the position where you can kill it, swiftly and humanely, this is the most effective. Unless, of course, you can afford to have a personal servant standing by to net it on your behalf.

Apart from my guy net, my preference in tackle is as idiosyncratic as that of any other salmon fisherman. I mostly use a two-piece Wye rod, eleven feet long,* with a 3¾ inch, Hardy Perfect Reel, Duplicated Mark II and a sink-tip line. The rod was originally designed for salmon-fishing on the restricted head-waters of the Wye River, and was very strong, but my two-piece version has been lightened down: I find it ideal for my Devonian purpose, and the stiffness of its action suits me very well. As to

Mid 19th c. salmon fly

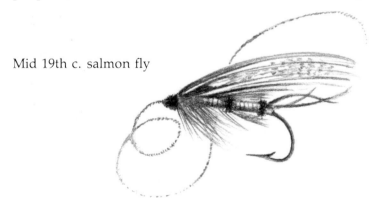

the line, I avoid the surface and sinking sorts, because the sink-tip, depending on where I lay my fly, allows me to fish high or low in the water at my discretion.

This sort of gear, uncomplicated and easy to carry, is all the itinerant Dartmoor salmon-fisherman needs. Compared with

---

*Bagged, in two 5½-foot sections, the rod makes an awkward load. But such a good rod is never a burden.

men going for carp, I travel very light. I enjoy being mobile, and free to fish anywhere, happily working my way downstream through all the possible pools and rocky crannies afforded by rivers of infinite charm and scenic variety. My pleasures are not confined to the pursuit of big fish: a day in the high summer, when the grilse* begin to run, can be as exciting as any other. These fish, four to seven pounds, will tend to lie in smaller pools; you can take them with lighter tackle, and you may find them in places far from the madding presence of anyone else.

Angling is a sport almost as old as historical times: its shades must be respected. Before you seek grilse, fresh-run, give thanks that you should have the chance to do so. Then ask, politely, of your guardian angel, for a bright day, alive with summer sun; a Devon river, in moderate spate; some peat in the moorland water, and health to fish it from early morning until late afternoon, with the prospect of a fish which, inch for silver inch, will fight as well as any other, apart, perhaps, from a large sea-trout.

In due time, if all this has been granted you, then you deserve more, since unto he that hath shall be given in abundance: namely, a grilse which has been in the river for a couple of days. This allows time for it to lose that layer of allegedly nutritious fat which it acquires after a year or so at sea. I find that fat oily and slightly filling: I prefer to have my fish like good beef, firm, lean, and properly cooked.

But 'properly' is a hard adverb to pin down. I have met Scotsmen who swear that salmon should be poached; Northumbrians who declare with equal fervour that it should be fried; Devonians who would have it grilled, while the mother of Richard Walker, in her *Sportsman's Cookbook*,* claimed that the

---

*Grilse are salmon which have spent only one sea-winter away from fresh water, usually in the Faeroes. They have therefore not put on as much weight as a fish which has spent longer at sea. In the past two years, in the South-West, I have seen large numbers coming upriver weighing only two or three pounds. No one can yet explain this.

*The Sportsman's Cookbook (Fish & Game) by Mrs. E.M.Walker, pub. Hutchinson/ Stanley Paul, 1978.

then editor of *Trout and Salmon* prescribed nothing more than simple, straightforward baking and serving with parsley sauce.

A plague, I say, on all of them. Anne does my catches in a large fish-kettle, letting the fish come to the boil for an instant and then gently simmering it in her own brand of stock, with wine, and bay leaves, and a squeeze of lemon, and love, and doubtless much else which she will not reveal, and I dare not try to discover. Sufficient that the ingredients of the stock may be varied, so long as the fish-kettle continues to be employed in the cooking: without that, no salmon can be accorded its honoured dues.

Salmon deserve those dues. No fish has been more lauded: no fish has been more avidly pursued. None of its breed is less than a worthy opponent, and all make fine eating. Peggy Howard, fisherwoman and cellist, used to serenade them (and was much surprised, one day, to hear the gruff tones of Sir Michael Hordern answering her aria from the opposite bank) for the sheer joy they gave her. And I am not alone among painters in never tiring of trying to capture them in pictures.

Kings and their courtiers, millionaires and bank clerks, captains of industry and their bench hands without distinction of rank or riches, have all been drawn to what is accounted 'the king of fresh-water fish'. Now, as did Walton some three centuries ago, 'people stand and wonder at the strength and sleight' by which they see a salmon go upriver.

No amount of farmed salmon (and over 25,000 tonnes will be produced this year) will ever take the place of the wild creatures which travel so far and return so doggedly. We need to conserve them, for our sake as much as theirs, to remind us of wonders and mysteries which we are in danger of overlooking. But we can conserve, and still catch: it is not anglers who are destroying them, for sensible fishing does no harm. The real damage comes from pollution, from overfishing at sea, and from those who refuse to abide by commonsense limits. A curse on all of them, for they may yet cast ruin on my ancient sport and deny to those who come after me the exquisite pleasure of this wonderful fish.

Glyn Lloyd-Jones, 'salmon man' with an 18½lb cock fish
from the Tavy

11
Envoi

Of the six great English rivers described by Izaak Walton in *The Compleat Angler* – the Thames, Medway, Tweed, Severn, Tyne and Trent – all have suffered to some degree from the march of 'progress'. Pollution has not been conquered: the evils men do to their environment live on.

Once, it was merely manufacturing industry which despoiled our rivers. In those rural parts where there were no factories, the water ran sweetly. Now, the most remote stream is at risk from even more insidious threats. The residues of agricultural pesticides and fertilisers run everywhere, and no one knows what their long-term effects on animals and plant life are likely to be.

Nowhere is safe. Many of the crustaceans in our estuaries are already suspect. Many of the fish in our inshore waters may soon need to be eaten with circumspection. The future of river-fishing, and rock-fishing, is by no means assured. A hundred years from now anglers may have to sit round concrete ponds, sanitised and sponsored by Tourist Boards with the approval of the Health

Inspectorate; with advertisements, perhaps, round the edges, like football grounds.

Victorian gentlemen were lucky enough to fish in habitats which were relatively unscarred. But they abused their good fortune by taking vast hauls of fish with very little regard to the future. All accounts of their grosser plunderings show salmon taken in quantities far greater than they, and their servants, could have possibly consumed. Much, in days when freezing was in its infancy, was clearly wasted.

I take no more than two salmon at any one time. I often take fish and put them back. I try to fish in ways which minimise the chances of line and hook being left in an escapee's mouth. In my work as a River-Warden, I do my best to serve the Water Authority's efforts to improve the riverine environment and to promote the future stocks of good fish. But in doing this, I am conscious that what I do, and what most good fishermen do, is not enough.

Historically, the Anglers' Cooperative Association has tried to fight off the pollution threat, but its task is daunting. Every day and in every way, things are going to become more difficult to control. More and more people live near rivers and keep boats on them; boats which spill oil and petrol; boats which are coated in anti-fouling chemical paints; boats from which too much rubbish is simply dumped over the side. More and more sewage, some of it untreated, is taken out (and often not very far out) to sea. More and more slurry and detergents and incompletely researched weed-killers soak, imperceptibly, into our rural watercourses.

On the high seas, stocks of commercial fish seem to be diminishing, ravaged by a minority of skippers who have no thought of tomorrow. I doubt if the richness of my youthful catches off Newhaven and Dungeness can now be so easily duplicated. The simple pressures of a bigger and very much more leisured and wealthy population bring doomsday more close.

But with care and concerted action and determination, the doom can be avoided: not easily, I admit, yet there are straws in the wind which blow towards some optimism. People are becoming more interested in their total environment, rather than the bit just outside their own back-yards. Commercial firms have more conservation-minded managers. Governments are made up from more conservation-minded Members of Parliament. It may take a very long time to clean up the past, but at least there are some signs that we are beginning not to defile the future.

The innocence of my teenage fishing days will not return. But if we take just a little care, there is no reason why many of our rivers cannot be saved for future fish-struck schoolboys. And, come to that, schoolgirls.

Angling, in whatever form, from chasing minnows with a jam-jar and net, to taking salmon on some splendid loch, is an art; a science; a splendid sport; and a noble way of life. I hope this book, in some small degree, has shown why, and wherein, lie the pleasures of which Walton wrote, so evocatively, over 300 years ago.

Index